Also by Peter Weddle

Work Strong: Your Personal Career Fitness System

Recognizing Richard Rabbit: A Fable About Being
    True to Yourself

Career Fitness: How to Find, Win & Keep the Job
    You Want in the 1990s

Generalship: HR Leadership in a Time of War

Postcards From Space

Being the Best in Online Recruitment
    & HR Management (2001, 2005)

'Tis of Thee

A Son's Search for the Meaning of Patriotism

WEDDLE's Guide to Employment Sites on the Internet
    (annually 1999-2004, biannually since 2005)

WEDDLE's Directory of Employment Related Internet
    Sites (annually 2002-2004, biannually 2005, 2007)

WEDDLE's Guide to Association Web Sites
    (biannually since 2002)

CliffsNotes: Finding a Job on the Web

CliffsNotes: Writing a Great Resume

Internet Resumes: Take the Net to Your Next Job

Electronic Resumes for the New Job Market

Computer-Based Instruction in Military Environments
    (with Robert J. Seidel)

What's This Book About?

Here's a sampling from the pages of *The Career Activist Republic*:

················· 🜨 ·················

Tens of millions of decent, dedicated and capable people—men and women who have successfully worked their entire lives—are now unemployed, unsuccessful in their search for a new job and unable to figure out why. No one has told them that the rules of the game have changed.

················· 🜨 ·················

As jobs drip-drip-drip out of the American workplace, every working man and woman feels as if they are being subjected to a brutal new form of torture—employment waterboarding. And, as the tenure of their employment continues to shrink in every corner of the work-place, they sense that they are being cast adrift by a new kind of environmental disaster—the national warming of work.

················· 🜨 ·················

The shrinkage of the job market has, ironically, made the talent of workers vastly more important to employers than it has ever been. … And their need—their desperate dependency—gives working men and women the power to control their own fate.

················· 🜨 ·················

But, what is talent? It is neither skill nor expertise. Talent is the capacity for excellence, and that gift exists in all people. In other words, the talent used to perform uncommon feats is no different from the talent used to perform even the most mundane deeds exceptionally well.

How do talented people go to work? The United States of America is arguably the most successful commercial nation in the history of the world, yet only a very small percentage of its citizens aspire to be business owners. In effect, *The Free Agent Nation* got it only half right: most Americans do want to work for themselves, but they want to be employed by someone else.

Career activists accept that they cannot trust their wellbeing to others; they understand that they cannot count on the self-anointed monarchs of Wall Street or the corner office grandees of corporate enterprises.

The Career Activist Republic resolves that dilemma. It replaces America's industrial era labor mentality with a modern marketplace—a 21st Century phenomenon—an economy of talent, by talent and with talent.

The trademark of career activists is a dedication to excellence—to using their talent to its maximum capacity on-the-job. They don't go to work as Me, Inc., but rather as Me™. And, that signature brand positions them as <u>the</u> extraordinary contributors in an organization.

Today, the American Dream is returning to its roots. It is (as it has always been) the freedom of each person to use their endowed talent in the pursuit of Happiness at work. It is the freedom they have to accomplish a single goal—to forge a future they cherish—by drawing on the genuine opportunity and enduring hope that happens only in the United States of America. That is their birthright, and its incarnation is the defining purpose of the Career Activist Republic.

for a bunch of old soldiers
you know who you are
Professionally Done

The
Career Activist
Republic

Peter Weddle

ISBN-13: 978-1-928734-54-3 / ISBN: 1928734545

A REPUBLIC

A state without a monarch—a political system in which the supreme power lies in the body of its citizens.

THE CAREER ACTIVIST REPUBLIC

An economic system without omnipotent employers—a workplace where the supreme power lies with people of talent.

What is occurring today
could only happen in the United States of America.
Its roots are the American birthright.
Its essence re-imagines the American Dream.

Table of Contents

Forward

A *major company workplace in the United States. The present day.*

Jeannette came into work on Monday, dreading the meeting with her boss. For months now—ever since the company's layoffs had started, in fact—Stiles had been dumping more and more stuff to do on her desk.

She wasn't resentful of the extra work—after all, everyone had to pitch in and do a little more during tough times. But, she did resent being mistreated. She had been hired to do one thing, and now, her boss—in his infinite wisdom—had her doing something completely different. She was able to handle the new tasks well enough, but that wasn't the point. The work didn't interest her or let her do what she did best.

The more she thought about it, the more it bothered her. Forcing her to work at what was best for the company regardless of what it did to her basically said she didn't matter. Who she was as a person and, just as important, her talent—what she was capable of accomplishing in the workplace—weren't of any consequence. It made her feel like an indentured servant. She was locked into a one-sided contract that pushed the company forward by pushing her down.

And, that wasn't the half of it. She might be willing to endure a lousy present if it gave her future some cover. But, the job security the company had promised ... well, it was a joke. No, it was worse than that. It was a sucker's sermon. She had believed in the company, trusted it, and counted on it. So did her friends and coworkers. They had all drunk the kool-aid. And what did they get in return? Execution by pink slip. At least a lot of them had.

They deserved better. A hell of a lot better, she fumed. This wasn't just mismanagement or inept leadership, it was torture. And no corporation,, no employer—not even a big, publicly traded, TV advertised, pundit celebrated one—should be allowed to …

… whoa, she told herself. Slow down. Getting yourself all riled up isn't going to make matters any better. And, it sure as heck won't help get you through the meeting with Stiles. Just take it easy. Hunker down and hang on. These days, that's the ticket to success—as pitiful as it is.

She took a deep breath and steeled herself for what was ahead. A minute later, the elevator door opened with a cheerless ping. She stepped out and headed for her desk.

The message light was blinking on her phone, but she ignored it. Dropping her purse and backpack by her desk, she headed for the coffee room. A little caffeine will get me ready for the hell-master, she thought to herself.

Halfway down the hallway, she heard her name bellowed from the corner office. The sound surged down the corridor and shoved her from behind. It was Stiles, of course, and his tone of voice left no doubt about his mood—foul as always.

"Jeannette," he roared again. "Where the devil are you? I want to do our meeting. NOW!"

Jees, Jeannette thought. It's not even 9:00 yet, and we aren't supposed to meet until 9:30. She shook her head in exasperation and turned around.

"Hey, boss. I'm ready if you are," she said as she turned the corner into the large, carpeted office. She purposely kept her tone upbeat, hoping to forestall yet another lecture about how everybody had to pull an extra load these days and that meant her, as well.

"Where have you been," the man demanded as he looked up with a scowl.

"I had us down for 9:30, so I ...."

"Your job is to be ready all of the time," he snapped. "I need to be out of the office at 9:30 so we're going to do the meeting right now."

"O.K.," she replied, keeping her voice positive. "Let me run back to my desk and get a pad."

"Go without," he growled. "If you come unprepared, you'll just have to make do."

Jeannette looked back at the man, and for the first time, realized the dilemma she faced. The situation was never going to change. It would never get any better. This man—her boss—was a bully and he would stay a bully until there was no one left for him to push around.

There simply was no possibility—not even the faintest hope—of relief. The company didn't care. In fact, it had promoted the cretin. Despite all the CEO's happy talk about seeing workers as its most important asset. Yeah right, maybe in my next life, she thought to herself. And the HR Department—when she told them about the problem—all they did was cluck in sympathy and wring their hands. So basically, she fumed, this was it. Working here was always going to be a legal form of adult abuse.

That realization brought her up short. She blinked as the impact of its clarity hit home. Suddenly, she could see the emperor without his clothes, and the sight made her want to gag. She recoiled and in the microsecond of that instinctive act of self-protection, her course was set. The motion was made, seconded, debated and approved before she was even aware she had done so.

Ten minutes earlier, she wouldn't even have considered it. But now ... now, everything was different. What she saw when she looked. What she thought and felt about what she saw. It had all changed. She didn't know where that change had come from, she wasn't even aware it had happened until, in the space of a gasp, it was there.

And now, it was shouldering its way into her consciousness like a subway rider on a crowded train. This change would not be pushed aside. It would not be ignored. But more than that. She could feel its presence with an intensity that shocked her. Its rightness disarmed her and overwhelmed her natural inclination to tread carefully.

She stood there for a moment and tried to make sense of it. She could see her boss talking at her, but his words were slamming up against a barrier that had somehow arisen in front of her. The magnetic poles of her perspective had switched, and for the very first time in her career, she felt as if she were protected. Safe. Shielded by a new and potent force field.

"Jeannette," her boss barked. "Are you paying attention to me? I'm not going over all this stuff to hear myself talk."

The man's voice rapped at her consciousness. But now, she could hear its hollow base. His words had lost their integrity, and that leached out their might. She looked down at him sitting behind his Maginot-like fortress of a desk and shook her head.

"Why are you shaking your ..."

Her vision was clear now. She could see behind the curtain. The man who had been the power in her career was a poser. He was nothing more than a role player, the Stepin Fetchit of a corrupt and corrupting way of managing people. And, she knew she deserved better. She deserved an employment experience that worked as well for her as it did for her boss and for the organization that employed her.

"Boss," she said.

"What," he replied. "What?"

"I quit."

She heard his jaw hit the desk as she turned on her heel and walked off.

M ost people would describe Jeannette's experience as a fairy tale. Who can afford to turn down a job in today's tough world of work? Countless Americans may fanaticize about doing what she did, but most have families to feed and a mortgage or a college fund to protect, so the prospect of facing down the tyrants at work is pure make-believe.

Or, is it?

A growing number of working men and women in the United States have begun to do exactly what Jeannette did. They are declaring their independence from workplace bullies and from employers that encourage and enable their malicious behavior.

More than that, though, they are pushing back at and pushing off from a way of doing business that promotes abusive employment. They are not doing so, however, in a blind rage or with reckless abandon. They are, instead, setting off with both a clear vision for what they want to accomplish and the necessary preparation for what they intend to do. They no longer have to tolerate being mistreated at work because they no longer fear the consequences of their rebellion. They have thought them through and carefully shaped them. They are Career Activists.

CHAPTER 1
The Age of Career Activism

The age of career activism is dawning in America. It is not yet fully formed—indeed, its final shape will likely take some time to emerge—but the forces that are propelling it have already begun to recast the American workplace. Their effects can be felt in Irvine and Indianapolis, in Chicago, Baltimore and Boston and everywhere in between. They are subtly, but inexorably forging a new contract between the country's employers and its working men and women.

THE GENESIS OF THE ACTIVISM

It took a Great Recession to unleash these forces. Americans were advised of their appropriateness, however, decades ago, in 1970. That year, the economist Milton Friedman wrote that a corporation's only responsibility is to its shareholders. Its only obligation is to increase its profits. A private sector organization may be composed of people, but it isn't responsible to or for them. Whatever may be written in its corporate handbook, whatever the Chief Executive Officer may opine on talk shows and in sugar-coated magazine articles, a corporation doesn't care about its employees. It isn't supposed to.

They must care for themselves.

Today's career activists are the protagonists of that sensibility. It is a radically ordinary concept, at least in the United States of America. Career activists accept that they cannot trust their wellbeing to others; they understand that they cannot count on the self-anointed monarchs of Wall Street or the corner office grandees of corporate enterprises. They acknowledge that they can and must depend upon themselves.

This reassignment of responsibility represents the leading edge of a revolutionary shift toward democracy at work. Career activists, however, are not striking for union representation. They are striking out on their own. They don't seek to establish a socialist economy. They are simply claiming their inalienable rights in the workplace. Their only objective is to represent themselves—to work as free and independent persons of talent.

A CORPORATE LEGACY OF ABUSE

Career activists are shaking off the indifferent paternalism of their corporate employers and stretching themselves to learn the ropes of enlightened self-interest. They are both moving to take on their responsibilities and pushing to be accorded their rights as American citizens in the workplace. They are asserting, not as an organized unit but as single workers of conscience, that they will no longer be employed where they are regarded and treated as 3/5 of a person. Some are Baby Boomers, others are Gen Xers and still others are Millennials, but all are taking a stand and refusing to be oppressed by an occupational system that mistreats them.

Are they being unreasonable? Is their view of corporate America inaccurate? Consider the facts:

- Historically, company layoffs were seen as a sign of poor leadership. Today's Wall Street whiz kids and hedge fund hotshots view such moves as smart management. They cheer when a company (other than their own) cuts its workforce.

According to researchers at the University of Illinois, corporations that laid off employees in 1985 saw their Fortune industry ranking slide by 1.3 positions. By 1994, the drop had declined to a negligible 0.24 positions. In 2009, a company's ranking might actually improve with the announcement of a corporate downsizing.

- The decade between July, 1999 and July, 2009 was a bonanza for corporate America and a bust for the country's working men and women. Although some companies struggled during the Great Recession, many employers were able to push their profits to some of the highest levels ever by using a strategy only tenured business school professors could cheer. They upped their productivity by downsizing 7.1 million workers.

  In the eight years since the 2001 recession, corporate profits doubled while the number of long term unemployed—those out of work for 27 weeks or more—rose to more than triple the unemployment rate. Without remorse or a second thought, corporate America lined its pockets while the American workforce stood in the bread line.

- At the same time, the income of the typical American household went down for the first ten-year period since the Great Depression. Investment bankers and business executives were buying condos and corporate jets while working men and women saw their homes foreclosed and their vacations canceled. In effect, the American Dream was running backwards.

  If a person went to work for the median U.S. income of $51,295 in 1998 and they were able to hang onto their job for the entire decade, they saw their earning power drop to $50,303 in 2008. Basically, they were working for the privilege of being poorer.

Given that kind of experience, it shouldn't come as any surprise that a growing number of Americans are taking their careers into their own hands. They are now charting their own destiny by declaring their independence from a system that denies them equality with the organizations that employ them, reduces their employment opportunity to the straight jacket of a corporate ladder, and uses the quarterly earnings statement to disenfranchise them from the American Dream.

THE STATE OF THE AMERICAN DREAM

How did we get to this point?

The United States of America is still the best place on Earth to craft a rewarding and fulfilling career. It continues to offer the best prospects for real and enduring success. It remains the most supportive of individual achievement and the attainment of personal prosperity. It is not immune, of course, to trying economic conditions, but those setbacks do not diminish its promise. The nation is today, as it has always been, a vibrant "land of opportunity." A place where hard work and talent can create both an extraordinary standard of living in the present and unfettered access to an even better tomorrow.

And yet, this vision—the American Dream—is now under attack. America's working men and women are taking up activism in the workplace because their future is at risk. In the space of a decade that straddles both the 20th and 21st Centuries, they have seen their self-confidence, their self-respect and their prospects assaulted by a double-barreled blast of corporate hegemony.

Instinctively, they sense the danger. Deep down in their gut, they can feel the threat. For some, it is too painful to discuss even with family and friends. For others, it is too depressing, too overwhelming to confront and rebuff. For still others, however—for a small but growing cross-section of the American workforce—it is a call to arms. It evokes a single, Bastogne-like response: Enough.

24

CHAPTER 2
A One-Two Punch to the Gut

H istory repeats itself, to be sure, but not always with the same consequences.

The Great Depression produced a number of fundamental changes in the values and outlook of the American people. It taught a generation or more of the nation's citizens to mistrust big banks, to depend first on themselves for meeting their personal needs and to minimize those needs by living frugally. These individual adjustments may initially have been ad hoc responses to a threatening situation, but they eventually became an ingrained way of life that continued long after the economy had stabilized and begun to grow again.

The Great Recession has produced a similar shift, among the American people to be sure, but also among American employers, as well. This economic shock lasted far longer (from December, 2007 until mid-to-late 2009) and was far more devastating than current business leaders had ever experienced (the U.S. stock market lost $6.9 trillion in value in 2008 alone—more than the entire U.S. budget in 2010). Corporate giants from General Motors to The Walt Disney Company, from United Airlines to eBay were left battered, weakened and struggling to adjust to their new circumstances.

In response, corporate executives have implemented a kaleidoscope of new policies, strategies and standard operating procedures. The specific adjustments and their implementation were obviously idiosyncratic to each organization. But for many, maybe even most, there is at least one change that is common. It is the abandonment of their traditional staffing practices. Seeking protection in an unfamiliar yet clearly less tolerant marketplace, a large and growing number of America's employers are now retooling the structure of work and the definition of employment.

FROM GONE WITH THE WIND TO 24

While the nature and scope of these adjustments are still being formulated by corporate executives, their impact on American workers is already beginning to emerge. They will, most career counselors and employment experts now agree, clearly increase the frequency of job change in America. Going forward, work will be a lot less like an epic drama and a lot more like a television series. It will shift the employment experience from *Gone With the Wind* to *24*.

This dramatically more episodic form of work will redefine what it means to have a career in the American workplace. The notion of a relatively stable and predictable job spent entirely with a single employer or even in a single industry or occupational field has, for some time, been a fast-fading memory from a slower and simpler economy. The new staffing actions employers are beginning to implement will now dramatically accelerate that transformation.

Instead of the 20th Century norm of 5 or 6 job changes over the course of a 30 or 35 year career, American working men and women will likely shuttle through 15 or more changes in employment. And, the nature of these moves will, themselves, be different. Historically, job changes often occurred within the same employer—a person was promoted or moved to a new assignment—and almost always within the same occupational field and industry. In the new world of work, a person's job changes will likely involve 10 or more employers in 3-to-5 industries and even 2-to-3 different occupations.

The shifting around will be continuous and touch virtually everyone in the workforce. The best evidence of this sobering new norm in employment is the situation already facing corporate chief executive officers. According to the executive search firm Spencer Stuart, the median tenure of CEOs in the S&P 500 is now down to just four years. That's barely enough time to get the corner office redecorated. And, if that's the emerging experience at the very apex of American companies, it will certainly become the norm throughout the rest of the organization, as well.

SEEDS OF CHANGE, SEEDS OF HOPE

This resetting of business as usual may serve the interests of corporate America, but to America's workers, it is a one-two punch to the gut of their future. It is an assault on each and every person individually and on the entire workforce collectively.

As jobs drip-drip-drip out of the American workplace, every working man and woman feels as if they are being subjected to a brutal new form of torture—employment waterboarding. And, as the tenure of their employment continues to shrink in every corner of the workplace, they sense that they are being cast adrift by a new kind of environmental disaster—the national warming of work.

Any change is jarring, but these changes are so extreme, they are rocking the foundation of America's sovereign self-confidence. For many, they have even sheared off the credibility of the American Dream. The steps now being taken by the nation's employers are leaving America's workers unsettled, unsure and, increasingly, unable to find their way forward in what is a workplace undergoing profound and seemingly incomprehensible revision.

Beneath the surface of this new and troubling employment landscape, however, seeds of hope are germinating. As difficult as the visible changes may be to understand and appreciate, they are nurturing the just emerging shoots of a positive transformation. They are pushing a truly liberating and beneficial epoch of employment up and out into the American workplace.

Though some may long for the more familiar circumstances of the past, this new period will not return the world of work to what it once was. It does not direct American workers back to where they were, but instead, frees them to move forward to what they can be. This fresh season of their possibility breaks through the stone-like restrictions that have long held the nation's workers down and blunted their natural growth and promise. It opens a new and more fulsome time of opportunity for America's working men and women.

CHAPTER 3
Employment Waterboarding

Unlike the ebb and flow employment pattern of previous economic downturns, the recessions of 1991 and 2001 subjected the U.S. to the horrible, hollow optimism and faux opportunity of a "jobless recovery." The economy expanded, but jobs were created at an almost imperceptible pace.

For example, according to the organization that dates business cycles, the National Bureau of Economic Research (NBER), the 2001 recession officially ended in November of that year. Yet, as 2003 drew to a close, payrolls and the jobs they supported among the country's employers were still declining. A full two years had passed, business profits were growing, and there were still legions of Americans out on the bricks looking for work.

Worse, that trend continued for almost ten years. Indeed, the decade between July, 1999 and July, 2009 was the first since the Great Depression to see virtually no new jobs added in America's private sector. The U.S. Bureau of Labor Statistics reports that during this period, job growth stalled at a puny 0.01 percent. That equates to a net gain of just 121,000 private sector jobs during the entire 10-year span, a figure that is only slightly larger than the crowd at a single Michigan State football game. As a result, those who were out of work continued to struggle to find employment even as business activity expanded. Employers were increasing production and service delivery, but they weren't hiring to do so.

B ad as that was, the job market after the Great Recession of 2008 has been even more radically transformed. Instead of experiencing a "jobless recovery," the country is now enduring its first-ever "less jobs recovery," a drip-drip-drip brutalization of workers that is unquestionably legal, but can only be described as employment waterboarding.

The economy is strengthening, but America's employers are still wrenching jobs and the people who fill them out of their organizational structure. They laid off over 1 million people between January and August 2009, 60 percent more than at the height of the recession in 2008. The economy has, by most measures, improved since then, yet the drip-drip-drip continues.

While economists predict that 2010 will produce 200,000 new jobs, employers' staffing announcements indicate that they will eliminate an even larger number of positions at the same time. Organizations ranging from the city of Fort Worth, Texas and Northern Arizona University to the J. Paul Getty Trust and NASA, from Microsoft and ON Semiconductor to Cessna Aircraft Company and General Motors have already said that they will continue to cut jobs into 2010, and those companies represent just the tip of the iceberg.

FROM LAGGARD TO LEADER

Pundits, of course, will opine that employment is traditionally a lagging indicator. It describes the impact of the past rather than the prospects for the future. That may have been so in the 20th Century, but in the 21st Century, exactly the opposite is true. Today, the nation's employment status is a leading indicator. The layoffs that are occurring now are the harbingers of more layoffs in the future.

For example, a 2009 survey by the HR consulting firm Watson Wyatt found that more than half of the nation's employers plan to decrease staff size over the next three-to-five years—the very same period economists predict the economy will recover. In effect, employers are finding ways to increase productivity and output, revenue and profits without adding to and, more importantly, while still cutting their workforce.

How are they doing so?

In many cases, the executives in those organizations feel safe in demanding more time and effort from their current (and often already overworked) employees. In other cases, they are (at long last) making better use of the technology in which they had previously invested. And in still others, they are simply shipping the work overseas where it can (allegedly) be done cheaper.

Whatever the approach, they are all energized by the same fundamental shift in the way organizations believe they should—and can—staff their operations. Today's workforce cuts are not your grandmother's layoffs. They are not temporary reductions in force; they are permanent reductions in structure.

Employers are not cutting back on the size of the workforce; they are cutting out entire chunks of the enterprise. Said another way, the jobs that are now being eliminated are gone forever. The economic recovery after this so-called Great Recession will not only fail to reinstate former jobs, it will actually continue to eliminate jobs that already exist.

THE UPSIDE TO ALL THE DOWNSIZING

This rapidly shrinking job market clearly poses a difficult challenge for American workers. Fewer employment opportunities means more competition for the jobs that do exist. It also reduces the available alternatives and thus the choice a person has among employers. It constricts the arc of possibilities available to them as they look for work that will challenge and reward them.

Despite these negative consequences, however, the diminution of the job market does have a positive aspect. There is an upside to all of the downsizing, not just for organizations, but for the first time, for the people who are affected, as well. The advent of a workplace with fewer jobs will actually upgrade the employment experience of America's workers. It will enrich their careers in a way that, heretofore, would have been all but impossible.

Historically, the rapid expansion of an employer's structure during periods of economic growth created a number of excess jobs. Certainly, that wasn't the intent, but it was the reality. In the rush to acquire enough capacity to promote, sustain and, if possible, accelerate business development, at least some positions of marginal utility were established and subsequently filled. They cropped up in middle management, but more often, they were found in the company's operational units where the pace was too frenetic and the expectations were too demanding for anyone to notice.

While this excess was clearly inefficient and costly, it did provide many organizations with a valuable strategic advantage. It gave them wiggle room or what business schools like to call "bench strength." Extra jobs and the additional workers they provided enabled companies to adjust rapidly to shifting market conditions and to exploit those windows of opportunity that give goose bumps to CEOs.

Today, that bench strength is thin to nonexistent in much of corporate America. It has been carved out of the organization and sloughed off in the detritus of the recession. What's left isn't a lean enterprise, it's a hollow one. And that unsubstantial state has forced employers to revalue the structure that remains. Ironically, by relying on fewer jobs, the titans of American business have made every job that does exist much more critical to their success.

Employers now need every box on the organization chart to make a real and meaningful contribution to their mission. For that to happen, however, those jobs must be filled with capable workers. The jobs themselves produce nothing, of course. It's the incumbents in those positions—the employees who do the work assigned to the jobs—that enable them to contribute to the organization's success. And the more able those incumbents, the greater that contribution.

The shrinkage of the job market has, in effect, made the talent of workers vastly more important than it has ever been. Employers no longer have room for "C" level performers and those who don't pull their weight on-the-job. They need champions in every profession, craft and trade they employ and the maximum output from every employee they hire. And that need—that desperate dependency—gives working men and women the power to control their own fate.

Employers are now as dependent on talent as professional sports teams. Those that can acquire an unfair share of talent—especially the best talent—will win, and those that don't will lose. It should come as no surprise, therefore, that a Business Roundtable survey taken in the fall of 2009 found that almost two-thirds (62 percent) of the companies that responded said they were experiencing "difficulty in finding qualified applicants to fill vacancies."

In the very same month, however, those same employers (and others) cut 55,679 jobs from their payrolls, effectively guaranteeing that those in the jobs that remained would be even more critical to their success. Employers believe they are now waging a fierce War for Talent, and month-in month-out, they are shooting themselves in the foot. They are downsizing themselves into an ever greater dependency on the talent of workers.

BUT WILL THE NEED BE ENOUGH?

Dependency does not automatically lead to opportunity. While talent has definitely become more vital for employers in the jobs they do have, the continuing reduction in the number of jobs clearly poses a threat to each individual worker. If the structure of employment in America has itself changed—if the country has entered an era of doing-more-with-less-jobs—there is the very real possibility that there won't be enough jobs to go around.

The land of the free and the home of the brave has for many of its citizens become an unpredictable place consumed with anxiety. Poll after poll in late 2009 and early 2010 found the American people looking over their shoulders in fear. *Time* magazine even described the post-recession workplace as a new 9/11 for America—an economy characterized by an unemployment rate that sticks stubbornly in the 9-11 percent range.

While that fear is deserving of respect—the current situation is indeed a time of relentless testing—its impact will not devastate the nation's inherent opportunity. The horizon of its frontier remains as vast and colored with hope as it has ever been. And already, the Great American Innovation Engine is starting to rev back up. It may take awhile to return to full throttle—after all, it's been idling in greed and consumerism for decades—but it is even now starting to vibrate again across the economy.

New ideas, new technologies, new industries, new products, new services are already cascading out of the minds, the creativity and the freedom of the American population. Some of these spring from the employees of major corporations—IBM, for example, was awarded 4,914 U.S. patents in 2009, more than any other company in the world. Others are created by inquiring minds in America's great research institutions—at the M.I.T. Media Lab, for example, they are now at work on over 300 inventions, ranging from sociable robots to stacking cars. Collectively, these creative efforts create both new jobs and revitalized futures for all of the country's working men and women. And that fertile capacity is unique to the United States of America.

What powers it—what is the planet's only renewable source of energy—is the heterogeneity of the American people. In the 20th Century, the nation learned it couldn't out-process the Japanese. In the 21st Century, it is learning that it can't out-produce the Chinese. But neither one of those homogenous nations can out-think, out-create, out-invent, out-innovate, or out-talent the American population. They are each a nation of one people. The United States of America is a nation of all the world's people.

When Americans refer to themselves, they acknowledge their roots—for those are their heritage—but always they complete their self-description with what unites them—for it is their future. They are Native Americans, English Americans, French Americans, Dutch Americans, Irish Americans, German Americans, Cuban Americans, Mexican Americans, Jewish Americans, Arab Americans, non-Ethnic Americans and yes, they are Chinese Americans and Japanese Americans too.

The American culture of acceptance, the American societal norm of integration, the American value of self-reliance, however imperfect, are today still singular beacons of hope and opportunity. Better than any other place on Earth, they light the way for those with a new idea, a different approach, a better solution. Only in America can a person join a republic where they will be challenged and pushed to their limits, but also welcomed for what they aspire to accomplish and revered for what they do. And, it is that extraordinary and irrepressible trait—that one-of-a-kind poly-tribal dynamism—which ensures there will always be an unquenchable need for talent in the American workplace.

CHAPTER 4
The National Warming of Work

E ven as the job market is dripping away, employers are also changing the way they fill the jobs that remain. There has been little or no notice given to this shift, and it is only just now coalescing into a strategy. Indeed, its early ramifications are likely to be hidden by staffing actions that appear normal and appropriate for the early stages of a recovery. They are, however, radically different both in their purpose and ultimately, in their effect.

Historically, America's employers, but especially corporate enterprises, binged on new hires when the economy was strong and purged those same employees as soon as it weakened. The strategy was oddly reassuring despite the disruption it imposed on working peoples' lives. It may have made for tough patches in their standard of living, but they had the security of knowing that there would always be an eventual return to regular employment and the quality of life it supported.

This bulimic behavior also had no downside for employers. They added capacity or cut costs as necessary to preserve their bottom line. Workers were a fungible resource that could be acquired and disposed of just like any other kind of corporate property. In fact, at least a handful of corporations actually moved the recruitment of employees into their Purchasing Departments, figuring their well oiled processes could achieve greater efficiencies.

Similarly, Bond, a British staffing firm apparently hoping to establish its bona fides with American employers, published a book in the U.S. in late 2009 entitled *Human Capital Supply Chain*. While not actually saying it, the premise was clear: people were nothing more than paper clips with personalities and could be managed that way. All you had to do was rack 'em, stack 'em and move 'em in and out the door.

Corporate leaders, of course, continued to lionize their employees in public, but their actions in private revealed a very different set of beliefs. They were P.T. Barnum reincarnate, and their oft-used barker's call—*our workers are our most important asset*—was actually a cynical code for the suckers they were making of their employees. Behind the pretty veil of caring, they and their bean counter cronies decided that they could and would limit the corporation's investment in its workforce to just that: verbal capital or what most people call *hot air*.

THE CORPORATE CURTAIN COMES DOWN

The corporate scandals of the early 21st Century began to weaken employers' ability to dissemble with their workers. Strategic blunders of monumental proportions in the auto industry, inept and even corrupt leadership in the insurance and healthcare industries, and breathtaking arrogance and misjudgments in the financial services and investment banking industries have pulled down the curtain behind which America's corporate leaders have long operated.

Today, the country's workers no longer assume that these executives know what they are doing or that they can be trusted. They no longer believe there is anything positive for them in the negative experience of traditional corporate staffing. All of a sudden, the rank and file in corporate America sees binging and purging for what it actually is: a bargain with the devil. Its illusionary security has finally been recognized as the faux benefit and real threat it is.

38

This tectonic shift in perception means that staffing bulimia is now as risky for employers as it is for their employees. It sullies their product and service brands in the marketplace and their corporate reputations in the media. It doesn't make them look cagy or smart, benevolent or "employee friendly." And, it obliterates their claim to good corporate citizenship and social responsibility (no matter how much money they send to starving people overseas).

Only among the isolated analysts of Wall Street is such behavior still celebrated, and while that may provide corporations with access to financial capital, it leaves them begging for human capital. Indeed, binging on and then purging workers now establishes those employers that practice it as the "worst places to work." And in today's interconnected world, that kind of rap quickly becomes viral and throttles their access to the top talent they need to succeed.

REDEFINING THE CORPORATE WORKFORCE

In response to this situation, a small but growing number of employers have begun—without fanfare or formal declaration—to alter the way they intend to structure and staff their organizations. The start point of this shift is not new—employers have tried it from time-to-time over the past several decades—but its end result will be dramatically unlike what has been tried before. Now, more than ever, employers are determined to effect real change in their human resource management.

They are not simply renaming the blocks on their organization charts as they did in the past; they are making a deep and fundamental revision to their conception of a workforce. Big no longer connotes success when times are good, and small no longer connotes it when times are tough. What these employers now seek is a steady-state minimization of their employee obligation. They are looking for ways to maintain staffing while managing employee expectations about the future. As the economy heats up, they seek to increase headcount even as they shrink the definition of employment, and that effectively produces a national warming of work.

As in the past, employers will start by identifying a set of positions they deem to be critical to the corporation's strategic success. They will segregate these jobs in the organization by defining them—informally in the near term but ultimately as a formal convention—as their core or "regular" structure. They are the tasks a company believes it must perform in order to ensure its successful operations in normal times.

When business expands, however, this capacity will become insufficient so employers will have to adjust. As they have in the past, some will continue their recessionary behavior and demand even more output from their current employees. Others may invest in more powerful technologies that can be rapidly installed and produce a quick increase in productivity. And, still others may opt to lease the capacity from other organizations by outsourcing certain functions or activities to them.

All of those strategies have limitations, however, so it's likely that the majority of employers will revert to old behavior and add to their structure. In previous recoveries, they would have accomplished this expansion by creating temporary positions that eventually become permanent jobs. In this PR-challenged environment, they will embark on a new approach, one that is much less blatantly injurious to workers. They will acquire capacity by adding structure, but this structure will not be considered core or regular. It will be viewed as a set of "reserve" positions that provide workers with full time but impermanent employment.

THE READY RESERVE OF CORPORATE AMERICA

Unlike traditional contract or temporary jobs—the realm of the free agent nation—these new reserve positions are not intended to accomplish a specific assignment or complete a discrete project. They will, instead, provide employment for workers who will toil side-by-side with those in the regular structure, but with the clear understanding that their tenure is subject to the always shifting (or impermanent) needs of the employer.

Employees in reserve jobs will be paid exactly as those in regular positions are. They will receive the same benefits as those individuals, and will likely be offered the same offices and cubicles, parking spaces and access badges. However, when the employer's needs (for whatever reason) make such positions irrelevant to its success, they will be quickly terminated and the positions eliminated.

This approach will not change the legal definition of labor categories, but it will transform the way employers manage their labor. They will be able to acquire the capacity they need without adding to their regular workforce. Terminations will still be difficult transitions for workers, but because they are no longer unexpected—because they are acknowledged as a possibility up front—they are likely to provoke less of the anger and subsequent brand damage that employee purging is now causing.

This structural transformation means that, for the first time, the regular or permanent workforce of many American employers will be smaller—often much smaller—than their reserve or impermanent counterpart. The classification of these workers will remain unchanged—they will all be full time employees—but for most of them, the tenure of their employment will be much shorter than they have ever experienced in the past.

Indeed, in a 2009 study conducted by the staffing firm Veritude, an astonishing 97 percent of the employers that responded said that they would not revert to their pre-recession staffing model once the crisis was over. And almost half (47 percent) said that other than permanent employees would play a larger role in their post-recession workforce. While some of those respondents were undoubtedly thinking of traditional temporary workers, many were clearly signaling a turn toward a reserve workforce.

41

THE NEW "HONEST TO GOODNESS, FULL TIME PERMANENT JOB"

The net effect of this shift will be to redefine the notion of "permanent employment." Traditionally, that's been the goal of most working Americans. They don't want to be card carrying members of the free agent nation and have to fend for themselves in the workplace. Quite the contrary. As an article in *The New York Times* in late 2009 put it, they seek an "honest-to-goodness, full time, permanent job."

For most of the late 20th Century, such a position may not have meant thirty years and a gold watch, but it certainly provided an employment experience that lasted longer than a couple of weeks or months. In the post-Great Recession era, in contrast, permanent will be much more fleeting for almost all workers. The tenure of reserve positions will be understood to end in three or four years and sometimes less. And, the tenure of regular positions, while longer—probably averaging six or seven years—will also have a recognized limit as employers' needs and strategies shift to accommodate the changes imposed by the ongoing evolution of the global marketplace.

Undoubtedly, this impermanence in the workplace will, at least initially, be extremely uncomfortable for a large segment of the workforce. Its advantage, however, is that it represents a much more honest form of employment than what has historically existed in the American workplace. The barker's call has been replaced with a more truthful message—*our workers are our most important asset, but only as long as we need them*—and that enables workers to protect themselves.

The one-way street of the traditional employment contract has been widened into a two-way thoroughfare. Now, both parties—working men and women and their employers—will enter into their arrangement knowing full well that it will last only as long as it benefits both the organization and the individual. There will be no winks and crossed-fingers about job security when job security is beyond the capability of every employer in today's global economy. There will be no expectations of unending employee loyalty when market dynamics preclude a reciprocal loyalty by the organization. There will be only a candid business relationship that offers no false promises or unrealistic hopes.

This new reality will be out in the open for all to see, and those who choose to do so will also be able to plan for and deal with it effectively. The termination of employment with an organization will no longer come as a bolt out of the blue, but instead be considered a routine event. It will not be a situation bathed in shame, but rather will be seen as a normal passage for almost everyone. And because it is anticipated and accepted, the movement this new arrangement causes is as likely to be initiated by the employee as it is by the employer.

In essence, workplace impermanence provides American workers with a built-in do-over. It installs a mechanism for revitalizing individual careers and the fulfillment they provide. It isn't strike three and you're out; its year three and you're on. The restless feet that settled the American frontier will now start to tame the American workplace.

For the first time, America's working men and women will be able to avoid the sheer mind-numbing boredom of working in the same role, performing the same tasks over and over and over again. They no longer have to turn the same bolt on the assembly line or shuffle the same papers in the office. Moving from job-to-job takes the drone-like monotony out of one's employment experience and replaces it with a stream of new challenges and opportunities. And, it's that unending revitalization which perpetuates the continuous improvement and growth that mark a person of talent.

AMERICA'S NEW EMPLOYMENT CONTRACT

This newly mutual awareness of job abbreviation effectively rewrites the employment contract in America. The 20th Century norm of an omnipotent organization dealing with a subservient worker will be replaced with a more sustainable arrangement between two equals. Just as corporate employers will add and subtract reserve positions and the talent which fills them, so too will employees go to work for and leave employers to suit their own career needs.

In the past, such continuous churn in one's work record was viewed as evidence of a lack of stability. It meant a person couldn't hold a job or worse, that they were undependable, disloyal or too uppity for their own good. So, employers branded such workers with a scarlet label. They called them "job hoppers."

A 2009 *Harvard Business Review* headline, for example, exclaimed "And they're still job-hopping," when noting that 20 percent of corporate America's best workers—those they call their *high potentials*—had "jumped ship" during the 2007-9 recession. The implication was clear. Something was terribly amiss in the workforce because the best and brightest were now deserting before the ship sank or whenever a better ship hove into view.

And, that self-reliant behavior is spreading into other segments of the population. More and more people are recognizing that constant movement is the only form of security in the 21st Century workplace. There never was any safety or even any stability in standing by an employer or hanging in there to help it out. Bulimic staffing saw to that.

Today, immobility is the new risky behavior. It threatens the progress of person's career and undermines the continuity of their employment. That's why the number of long-term unemployed workers is now at its highest level in recorded American history. And, that's also why those high potentials the *Harvard Business Review* was clucking about took matters into their own hands.

The only way working men and women can protect themselves from the continuous change in the modern American workplace is to stay ahead of it. Each person must put change to work for them. Each individual must set themselves in motion—choosing the direction and course the change will take. Each must become the proactive master of their career so they don't end up its passive victim.

CHAPTER 5
The American Choice

America's employers have long trumpeted the value of their workers. Senior executives wax eloquent in press reports and interviews about the critical role their employees play in the organization's success. Their favorite descriptive term is "asset"—subtly signaling that they own those who toil for them—preceded by some superlative adjective such as "the greatest," "most important," or "prized." It is high praise, and it is a sham.

Traditionally, these statements have been interpreted to mean that America's employers truly recognize and appreciate their employees. While that view was debatable in the 20th Century—you don't toss out assets the minute the economy dips—it is unquestionably false today. The narrative is now nothing more than a public relations ploy and bears no semblance whatsoever to how employees are actually treated inside a company.

The "less jobs recovery"—a new world of work where economic growth is accompanied by organizational constriction—has reset the purpose of corporate staffing. Employers are no longer content to hire a normal distribution of workers—a few "A level" performers, a few "D level" performers and a lot of those who do enough at the "C level" to get by. They seek, instead, to employ as much talent as possible. They want to arrange for the daily delivery of excellence on-the-job.

> **T**hat transaction between a buyer and seller of talent—not a buyer and seller of labor—is the essence of the new employment contract in America. A worker who is qualified for an organization's opening—the conventional definition of what employers have sought when recruiting a new hire—is no longer viewed as sufficiently capable to meet the demands of a highly competitive global marketplace. Organizations now want someone who is accomplished at work—a person who can and will make a significant contribution on-the-job.

A PROSPERITY OF TALENT

This new approach is an extension of an old strategy. It mimics the way organizations have always hired their most senior employees. Employers view such individuals and CEOs, in particular, as high impact talent. They need them in order to succeed, and they're willing to pay to get them.

Since 1976, CEO compensation—not including their benefits and pension—has increased by a breathtaking 223 percent. Today, the leaders of America's largest companies take home an average of $8 million a year, after adjusting for inflation. And, that figure is going up as the recovery from the 2008 recession takes shape, and businesses prepare for growth and the rise in profits it typically generates.

How do companies justify such lofty compensation? What rationale do they offer given that the U. S. Bureau of Labor Statistics has reported exactly the opposite trend for the rest of the workforce? How can corporate Boards of Directors pimp the worth of CEOs while depressing the wages of their organizations' non-management workers by 10 percent during the same period?

The explanation can be reduced to a single word: talent. Companies believe that the talent CEOs bring to work each day is both critical to the organization's success and in critically short supply. They are, in essence, all stars. And, the only way to recruit and retain such individuals is to pay them handsomely. While their tenure on-the-job is no longer guaranteed or even expected to last very long, those who meet or exceed their performance goals (and all too frequently, even those who don't) will be very well compensated.

In effect, survival of the fittest has been replaced by a new law: "prosperity of the talented." And today, this neo-Darwinian dictate is no longer limited to those at the most senior levels. It is now percolating down into the middle and even junior ranks of many organizations. Indeed, talent is now viewed as the critical energy source—the clean power—of the 21st Century corporation. Without it, employers cannot move forward. And, those who have the most of it will speed by everyone else in the global marketplace.

Corporate America's more intensified appreciation for talent— "human capital" being such a quaint and misleading term—has led many employers to adopt a new approach to human resource management. Unlike what one might expect, however, this shift does not establish a more perfect employment situation for America's workers. Instead, it has produced exactly the opposite. It has left the nation with a meaner workplace.

Employees may never have really been treated as assets, but today, they are managed as statistics. Without any explanation or notice, companies have begun to prune their ranks of employees who are deemed to have less talent and to limit their hiring to only those who are perceived to have the most talent. It is fantasy sports team management for real.

A CHANGE IN THE RULES OF THE GAME

The term of art for this new approach is "quiet recruiting." Even as employers continue to slim down their structure and lay off excess employees, they are silently trading out less capable workers for those with more perceived value.

> - **In some cases, that value is acquired through "bargain staffing." Employers simply hire an often younger and less experienced person who can do (or be taught to do) much of what an often older and more experienced person would accomplish, but at a much lower salary.**
> - **In other cases, the value is acquired by "all star staffing." Employers trade out those in their workforce who are perceived to be "C level" performers (or worse) in order to adjust their structure and hire individuals with a track record of "A level" performance.**

Regardless of the approach they use, however, employers have to be careful not to trigger an equal opportunity/affirmative action audit from the Federal Government. To protect themselves, therefore, they redefine the openings created by their terminations to require incumbents with less experience or seniority in the case of bargain staffing and more capability or talent in the case of all star staffing.

Although seldom formally acknowledged, bargain staffing has always been a part of the American workplace. If offshoring moved work to less expensive labor overseas, such "downcosting" moved it to cheaper employees right here at home. It is an insidious and often illegal strategy, but one that can effectively pare payroll and benefit expenses. Hence, employers consistently disclaim any allegiance to age bias, but all too often practice de facto ageism in their staffing.

What's new in the post-Great Recession era, therefore, is all star staffing. For the first time ever, many companies are now hiring rank and file workers with the same score card and tactics they have long used to hire their most senior executives. They are no longer content with a normal distribution of capability; they want, instead, to skew toward a preponderance of accomplished workers.

On the surface, that strategy would appear to be beneficial for America's workers. In reality, it's quite the opposite. Tens of millions of decent, dedicated and capable people—men and women who have successfully worked their entire lives—are now unemployed, unsuccessful in their search for a new job and unable to figure out why. No one has told them that the rules of the game have changed.

THE GROWING DEMAND FOR TALENT

In the past, employers were willing to hire those who had modest skills and train them to perform a job. Today, they will only employ individuals who have all of the skills to do a job and the state-of-the-art knowledge required to use those skills effectively on-the-job. In the past, employers were happy to hire qualified workers to fill their open positions and accepted that only a few would exceed their expectations, most would meet them, and the rest would need remediation and support. Today, they seek the truly accomplished to do a job, and they expect superior performance from them and from their first day of work.

Only a person of talent can measure up to such a standard. They alone satisfy one or both of the two criteria employers use to identify an accomplished worker:

- **They have a skill that is critical to organizational success and a track record which demonstrates their ability to use that skill effectively on-the-job.**

and/or

- **They perform at a superior level on-the-job which enables them to make a significant contribution and set a standard that encourages their coworkers to excel at their work, as well.**

Increased demand for talent has not, however, increased employment. Even though millions of Americans are now in the job market looking for work, a large percentage of employers believe there is a shortage of talent in the workforce. While their email boxes and mailrooms are filled to overflowing with resumes, they see themselves as increasingly challenged to find, recruit and retain workers who have a track record with critical skills and/or the commitment to superior performance necessary for organizational success in the global marketplace.

In essence, employers are convinced that only a very few people have talent and that talent is, therefore, in critically short supply. While this view is their accepted wisdom, it is actually only half right. The truth is that every human being is born with a talent—it is an inherent attribute of the species—but, sadly, only a very small percentage of people actually work with that gift. And because so few American workers build their career on their talent, there is—for the moment, at least—a real and persistent shortage of that organizational energy source.

THE SHORTAGE OF TALENT

Today's talent shortfall has its roots in two developments that have significantly affected the American workplace over the past quarter century or so. One involves a change in the kind of capability American employers need, while the other requires that American workers use their talent in a new and different way.

The First Development

The role of technology changed dramatically during the last two decades of the 20th Century and the first decade of the 21st Century. It became a much more important part of how work was accomplished in both the production of goods and the delivery of services. Tens of thousands of organizations purchased a host of new hardware and software systems, including those for computer-aided design and manufacturing; data storage, processing and analysis; and internal as well as external communications. They put robots on the assembly line, computers on middle managers' desks, automated tellers in banks and self-serve scanners in the checkout line of grocery stores.

Initially, the vast majority of companies had only a minimal if any understanding of how best to leverage this technology to their best advantage. By the mid-to-late 1980s, however, many organizations had figured out that the technology, itself, was worthless—just a bunch of expensive silicon wafers and 1s and 0s—without skilled employees who could put it to work on-the-job. To capture the process, productivity and quality gains locked within their hardware and software systems, employers had to hire the people who had the ' talent to deploy, integrate, operate and maintain their technology investments.

The significance of that realization is best illustrated by the contrast between two commercial airline flights in 2009. Both flights occurred in identical state-of-the-art aircraft—the Airbus A320—yet the journeys produced markedly dissimilar outcomes. Thanks to the talent of its pilot, Chesley "Sully" Sullenberger, U.S. Airways flight 1549 survived a crippling bird strike and a dangerous water landing to become "the miracle on the Hudson." Northwest Airlines flight 188, on the other hand, had a very different caliber of pilot at the controls—one who was qualified, but lacked a commitment to excellence—so it lost radio contact with air traffic controllers for over an hour and overflew its destination by 150 miles. The basis for the vastly different results—the tipping point between success and failure—was the talent of each organization's employees.

Captain Sullenberger was not only a talented pilot, he knew how to use his talent effectively with the technology of his job. In effect, he made the plane perform up to his personal capacity for excellence. The Northwest pilot, on the other hand, knew how to fly a plane, but he didn't bring his talent to work with him. As a consequence, he brought the plane's performance down to his own level of mediocrity.

The Second Development

The past thirty years also saw a new generation of non-U.S. companies begin to compete with American businesses in both domestic and international markets. From cars to data processing, from kitchen appliances to home furnishings, from financial services to fashion, America's manufacturers and service providers no longer held an unchallenged position among their native customers. All of a sudden, the land of opportunity was open to the likes of Ikea and Toyota, Virgin Atlantic Airways and Sofitel.

This radically more competitive and pan-national economy forced chess-like adjustments in product and service design and delivery as well as corporate strategy and operations. The way organizations worked began to change and then changed again and again and again. As a result, employers needed workers who had the flexibility and creativity to contribute with impact—to perform at a high level in a highly dynamic environment and to do so from day one. Companies could not meet their business goals—indeed, they could not even survive—with workers who were stuck in ruts or unwilling to adapt to changing circumstances. They needed men and women who were able to deliver a valuable result on-the-job even as the requirements and responsibilities of that job were changing.

The movie actress Lillian Gish is a perfect illustration of what they were looking for. She began her career in 1912 in silent movies. Acting in such films as *The Birth of a Nation* and *The Scarlet Letter*, she applied her talent in a medium without sound by using carefully choreographed gestures and exaggerated facial expressions. Her ability to communicate without words made her one of America's best-loved actresses, and then, all of a sudden, the job of acting changed forever. The technology of sound was introduced.

Many of Gish's fellow actors were unable or unwilling to adjust, but she did. She adapted her acting style to the new requirements of the workplace and, equally as important, trained herself to excel in that medium. Her flexibility and capability enabled her to act for 50 more years and earned her an Academy Award nomination for her role in the 1946 move *Duel in the Sun*. In 1971, almost 60 years after she began her acting career without saying a word, she was honored with a Special Academy Award "For superlative artistry and for distinguished contribution to the progress of motion pictures"—progress that was built on continuous change from silent to sound, black and white to color, realism to animation and galaxies far, far away.

THE WAR FOR TALENT

The 2009 survey by Veritude (see Chapter 4) underscored the power of the new talent imperative. While 62 percent of the human resource and procurement officials it surveyed had laid off employees in response to the recession, even more were doing so to improve the capability of their staff. An astonishing 63% of the respondents acknowledged that they were letting average performers go and creating new positions that only accomplished persons could fill. They weren't using the downturn to upgrade the workforce they had; they were using it to trade up to an entirely new caliber of worker.

Even executives weren't immune from this trend. A survey of employers conducted by ExecuNet, a career management support company for senior professionals and managers, found that half of its respondents (49.5 percent) intended to "trade up" with their new hires in 2010. They did expect to add new managers and supervisors to their staff, but they were no longer searching for a round peg who would fit into a round hole. They had eliminated the hole altogether and were looking, instead, for someone who could stand out on their own.

In the space of just three decades, employers reset their hiring priority from those with industrial era skills and a do-the-job mentality to those with information era skills and a make-the-maximum-contribution attitude. They are no longer in the business of employing workers who are loyal and hardworking. They still value those characteristics, to be sure, but to survive, they must now hire a different breed of person—one who knows how to use their talent effectively in the modern workplace and is committed to doing so.

Historically, American employers have always enjoyed a surplus of labor. Thanks to the appeal of the American Dream, the country has been blessed with a continuously replenished supply of people who had or could acquire 20th Century skills and were hardworking and loyal employees. Corporate America's shift to hiring workers for today's more technology-dependent and competitive economy, however, has created a serious supply-demand mismatch. Employers are now realizing that there is an insufficient number of workers who have both 21st Century skills and a commitment to excellence. They still have a surplus of manual labor, but they are in critically short supply of talent.

A report by the consultancy McKinsey & Company published just three years before the end of the 20th Century, gave a name to this new environment. They called it a War for Talent. The American workforce lacked enough persons of talent—those with a track record in critical skills and/or a commitment to superior performance—to go around. From now on, the report warned, employers would have to fight over the talent that is available. And, the definition of victory in that battle is an organization's ability to capture an unfair share of such workers.

As it is with their chief executive officers, the corporate strategy for winning the talent war depends, in large measure, on financial incentives. While never on the same scale as that used with their senior executives, corporations have now begun to invest much more money to recruit and retain people of talent throughout the ranks. Often these sums are substantial and significantly greater than what they are willing to pay to other employees. In effect, organizations have replaced their historically egalitarian approach to compensation— where "A" level performers received raises that were only marginally better than "C" level performers—with an approach that is decidedly more meritocratic and market-based.

PAYING UP FOR TALENT

The baseline for this adjustment was, from the corporate perspective at least, felicitously low. Over the past twenty-five years, the compensation of most workers barely kept up with the pace of inflation. In fact, for the first time since the U.S. Government began tracking such figures, the household income of working Americans actually declined in the decade between 1999 and 2009.

Over the first five years of the 21st Century, the total remuneration of America's working men and women—their take home pay and benefits—plummeted to just 56 percent of the country's gross domestic product. That level is just 7 percent better than it was in 1929, when the country entered the Great Depression.

Even as this compensation catastrophe was unfolding, however, the situation was very different for those workers who were deemed to have talent. As shown in the table below, these individuals saw employers increase the financial incentives they offered both to recruit them—by paying hiring bonuses and above market salaries—and to retain them—by making market adjustments to their pay to keep it competitive with their peers and by offering special bonuses to keep them in place. For perhaps the first time ever, American employers began to invest in talent as if it actually were what they had always been calling it—an asset.

Number of Employers Offering Special Pay for Talent

Pay Adjustment	2004	2008
Hiring bonuses	61%	70%
Market adjustments	55%	65%
Retention bonuses	27%	38%
Paying above market	25%	31%

Today, employers are so desperate for talent—so sure that it is absolutely critical to their organizational preservation and prosperity—that they will pay dearly to acquire even discredited individuals as long as they can deliver results on-the-job. The 2009-10 debacle in the financial services industry is a case in point. Struggling banks, brokerages and insurance companies were convinced that they had no choice but to pay huge salaries and even larger bonuses to the investment gurus who created the credit default swap fiasco in the first place. Ironically, only those individuals had the know-how to undo the mess they had created so their employers were not only willing, but were determined to pay them whatever it took to keep them on-the-job.

Even more dramatic, employers have made all star staffing a central element of the way they manage all of their human resources. They now operate much like professional sports clubs. Those organizations may brand themselves as teams, but they have long operated as businesses. They are constantly adjusting their mix of talent—by the hiring, trading and firing of players—in order to enhance their ability to compete. They owe it to their fans, they argue, to upgrade their roster each and every year because that's the only way to ensure victory on the field.

In a case of life imitating sports, corporate employers are now doing exactly the same thing. They are quietly, sometimes even surreptitiously, using the recession to trade up for workers who have stronger skill sets and/or better track records of performance. They have ditched the normal distribution of talent in their workforce and are now trying to field their own brand of a dream team.

NO CHOICE BUT TO CHOOSE

This new talent imperative is quietly but inexorably sweeping through the American business community. Although its influence is already reshaping the employment experience of countless workers, it is not yet recognized by many of them. In essence, those who are most affected by the change are the ones who are least aware of it.

That lack of recognition does not, however, diminish the inherent challenge of this new dynamic. Today's leaner and meaner workplace leaves America's working men and women with only two options. And because the change around them will not stop or even pause, they have no choice but to choose the one they will pursue.

America's workers can passively accept this new world of work and submit themselves to whatever consequences it may impose. They can ignore their talent and surrender their future to haphazard opportunities and progress by chance. And, they can turn their backs on their capacity for excellence and watch their standard of living decline as their career careens from one unrewarding role to another.

Or, they can proactively confront this new environment and forge a course of action that works for them. They can claim their inalienable right to equality with employers in the American workplace. And, they can secure that claim by establishing themselves as career activists—people of talent who are the free and independent citizens of the modern workplace.

There is no other option. And making no choice is a choice—it is choosing to give in. Every American worker now has to set the course of their career or have their course set for them. They can reclaim the American Dream or let it fade away. The decision is theirs. Theirs alone. Only they can make it. And they must.

CHAPTER 6
The Career Activist Republic

The common understanding of talent limits it to exceptional people who engage in exceptional activities. According to this view, only a very few individuals have talent, and their talent is expressed in only the most rarified of fields and feats. People of talent are professional athletes, entertainers and artists. An opera singer at the Metropolitan Opera in New York City has talent while the best a bank teller or a plumber can be is good at their job. Talent, Americans are taught and told, isn't something the masses have, nor is it really talented to be an exceptional performer in unexceptional occupations.

THE CONVENTIONAL ELITISM OF TALENT

Ascribing talent to only a select few is a pretension that strikes at the very heart of human equality and the American democracy. This elitism of talent has its roots in the industrial era. In the early decades of the 20th Century, mass manufacturers—most notably those that produced cars and food—needed workers who would labor as machines or beasts of burden and perform the same tasks over and over again. To legitimize this drone-like existence, the social arbiters of the time created the conceit of America's "unwashed masses" to set common people—the working class—apart from their more educated and cultured betters. It was a derogatory description with synonyms like "migrants," "rabble" and "wage slaves."

Not to be outdone, the country's academic establishment reinforced the talent divide by introducing a developmental structure and programmatic format designed to relegate all but an exceptional few to mediocrity. Called "gifted and talented" programs in elementary school and "advanced placement" in high school, these initiatives didn't just serve the needs of smart kids—an admirable goal. They also communicated a sense of inferiority to all those who were not selected. In effect, the "normal" kids were told they didn't have talent or advanced capabilities and thus were second class citizens in the nation's educational system.

The Duke University Talent Identification Program, for example, describes itself as "a global leader in identifying academically gifted students and providing them with innovative programming to support their development." In other words, a person isn't talented unless they are academically gifted. If a kid doesn't score high on some so-called "intelligence test," they aren't smart enough to do extraordinary things in life and thus should receive only uncreative programming and support.

Even Google, allegedly one of the world's most democratic search engines, mirrors this bias. Type the word "talented" into its search box, and the first ten results range from Susan Boyle and Britain's Got Talent to the National Research Center for the Gifted and Talented. Perform the same search with Microsoft's Bing and the results are different but not different in kind. They include the Talented Mr. Ripley and TalentEd, a site "dedicated to the provision of material about the education of the gifted and talented."

Similarly, television shows such as America's Got Talent and contests such as the Intel Science Talent Search signal that talent is something reserved for only those fortunate enough to have an uncommon skill or capability—people who are more analytical, athletic, or musically inclined than everyone else. They are rappers and rocket scientists, pianists and physicists and their peers. The rest of the population does not measure up and is, therefore, considered untalented.

A MORE PLURALISTIC PERSPECTIVE

The dictionary, thankfully, takes a more pluralistic view of talent. It defines the word as "the natural endowments of a person" and then defines an endowment as "a natural gift, ability or quality." There is no qualifier limiting talent to extraordinary people or to extraordinary endeavors. The term is not reserved for the infallible and famous or even for the in-your-face and infamous. Quite the contrary, talent is a natural characteristic of the human species and is expressed in the full range of its idiosyncratic interests and occupations.

There is talent in being an exceptional salesperson and extraordinary truck driver. Talent can be expressed by an especially good customer service representative and bank teller, and by a truly outstanding electrician, mechanic, carpenter and computer programmer. The talent is not in what a person does, but in how they do it. Talent, then, is the expression of excellence, and that excellence can be attained in any and every profession, craft and trade.

In addition, the contempt with which many traditional talent elites are now held among the general public has further undermined their claim to specialness. Thanks to athletes who use steroids to set records, entertainers who indulge in sophomoric behavior to make headlines, business and investment gurus who commit criminal acts to enrich themselves, and politicians who can't seem to act at all despite the pressing issues of our day, people simply no longer believe that those who have traditionally been viewed as being talented are also extraordinary beings. Despite the nation's tabloid fascination with them, most Americans have concluded that talent elites are no better and often much worse than everybody else. And since that's so, the rest of the population is just as likely to have talent as the so-called superstars are.

This shift in perspective recasts talent as a trait that:

- all people possess, regardless of their social standing, fame or fortune;

and

- each and every individual can use to be accomplished in their life's work.

These two principles undergird the democratization of talent. They form the foundation for a new movement in the American workplace. Called the Career Activist Republic, this emerging culture affirms the nobility of all human work and of all of those who perform it. It recognizes that, despite the differences among Americans in their ethnicity, gender and national origin, they are all equal persons of talent. Each and every one of them.

The Career Activist Republic has its roots in the founding beliefs of the American democracy. Despite that heritage, however, its respect for the universality of talent and the right of every person to use that talent in their work will not be automatically recognized or accepted in the workplace. That view undercuts the cozy advantage enjoyed by employers in 20th Century American capitalism, and those employers are loath to lose their upper hand. The determination to achieve equality at work is, therefore, the defining attribute of the Republic's citizens. It is what makes a person of talent a career activist. They are ordinary people who are pledged to claim their endowment—their talent—in their work, their jobs, and their career.

Their activism has been triggered by the leaner and meaner workplace of 21st Century America. It draws its strength from a unique mixture of the human urge to explore—in this case, themselves—

and the rebellious independence that oxygenates the American culture. It represents the American worker's rejection of the "separate and unequal" doctrine of the country's talent elites and their determination to establish a true democracy of talent.

A DEMOCRACY OF TALENT

While talent is a universal attribute, it is not universally used. There are some who ignore their talent because they don't believe it can support a standard of living that is acceptable to them, and there are others who abuse their talent by refusing to nurture and develop it to its fullest potential. What separates the career activist from others, therefore, is their decision to express and experience their talent in the one-third of their life they spend at work.

That commitment, in turn, is the reason the community of career activists is a republic. Such an assembly is generally defined to have two key attributes. A republic is:

- A state in which the supreme power rests not with a monarch, but in its citizens;

and

- A body of persons freely engaged in a specific activity.

Hence, the Career Activist Republic is composed of men and women who:

Reject the supreme power traditionally accorded to employers in the American workplace.

The American legal system may have historically empowered employers to act as monarchs—"at will employment" gave them the authority to hire and fire workers whenever it suited them—but today's market reality—with its severe shortage of excellence in the workforce—enables workers to act as the equal of any organization that hires them.

Career activists do not recognize or accept the superiority of employers and demand, instead, that they and those they represent—the persons of talent of the United States—be accorded their full rights of citizenship in the workplace as well as in their community and government.

Accept personal responsibility for the direction and care of their own careers.

The American economy may have historically forced workers to rely on their employers for the management of their careers—the career ladder gave them no choice in either the extent or pace of their progress—but today's global marketplace—with its unpredictable and turbulent business conditions—liberates workers to act as the masters of their own destiny in the workplace.

Career activists do not want or need any organization or organizational representatives—be they their boss or the HR Department—to shape their future and believe, instead, that it is both their obligation and their uniquely American opportunity to define and achieve their own Dream.

Commit themselves to the fullest possible development and use of their talent.

The American culture may have historically excluded its workers from any claim to talent—the nation's incessant lionization of sports and entertainment figures all but drowns out the achievements of others—but today's War for Talent—with its utter desperation for talent among America's employers—resets workers' self- respect and encourages them to nurture the capability with which they have been endowed.

Career activists recognize that their claim to full citizenship in the workplace depends upon their unflagging commitment to becoming and then performing as a person of talent and, through that expression of their special gift, to contributing as best they are able to their employer's mission.

IS SUCH A REPUBLIC SELF-DEFEATING?

On its face, the Career Activist Republic seems to be a self-defeating proposition. If the Career Activist Republic is based on a shortage of talent, that shortage seems destined to dissolve as more and more people join the Republic. The independence and advantage that people of talent will enjoy in this new democracy are, according to this logic, likely to be lost if everyone else is just like them—if all Americans commit to developing and using their talent. Like a latter day Madoffian bargain, the success of the first career activists will attract more converts, and their numbers will inevitably dissolve the shortage and make success impossible for everyone else.

While such a scenario has a definite whiff of reason to it, there are at least two reasons why it is unlikely to occur. First, not every American will elect to become a member of the Career Activist Republic. Some will be too fearful and others too lazy. They will claim the Life and Liberty the country affords them, but hold back from their pursuit of Happiness. They will consign themselves to a 30- or 40-year stretch in one of life's most oppressive prisons: a boring career. They will ignore their individual talent and collectively preserve the shortfall of talent in the workforce.

Second, talent is the Holden Caulfield of economics. It is every economist's worst nightmare. Talent doesn't follow the "rules" of marketplace manners. It doesn't behave like a good little resource. In fact, even if every working American suddenly joined the Career Activist Republic and even if every immigrant and new citizen also signed on—even if the supply of talent increased by an order of magnitude—there would still be a desperate need for talent in the workplace.

This seeming contradiction in capitalism is caused by the nature of talent. It is true that, as many Americans have learned over the past twenty-five years, the way a specific talent is used can become obsolete. The introduction of new technology, the shifting interests of consumers, the decline of mismanaged corporations and the rise of cheaper or more productive competitors can transform a talent's application that was once in great demand into one that is no longer needed or valued. That's what happened to those whose expertise was devoted to textile manufacturing, data processing and mid-level management. Factors beyond their control blind-sided their careers and all but pulled the American Dream from their grasp.

Human beings, however, are not buggy whips or black and white television sets (unless they choose to be). As obvious as that statement may be, the distinction is worthy of note. Unlike what happens with inanimate resources, a change in marketplace demand does not render a person's talent worthless.

The factors that are beyond their control do not leave them out of control in their career. Technological, marketplace and other developments do not occur overnight, but rather over a period of time and sometimes even over several years. And, that delay in impact gives a career activist the window of opportunity they need to make the necessary adjustments in their career.

Those adjustments are possible because talent is not skill. Talent is an inherent capability—an endowed capacity for excellence—which can be taught to do several kinds of work. No talent is compatible with all work, but every talent can be expressed in more than one career field. It can be trained to perform as one skill today and another skill tomorrow. It is flexible, adaptable and highly susceptible to learning.

Talent, then, is the universal donor in the workplace. It can be used effectively almost anywhere. The ever-changing landscape of the modern workplace ensures that employers' demand for specific skills is always in flux. Their need for talent, however, is constant and enormous.

That reality provides career activists with two alternative courses of action when the market no longer values their particular application of talent:

- In some cases, the situation may warrant a change in degree rather than in kind. In other words, while the demand for the current application of their talent is down, it is not completely eliminated. Therefore, a career activist can reinforce their expertise and upgrade their performance to a level that will sustain their employment despite the lower demand. In effect, they act to remain an all star, but in a smaller league which still offers them opportunity and security.

- A career activist can also apply their talent to another field of work. They can transfer their inherent capacity for excellence to a different occupation or industry. For example, someone whose talent is persuasion—the ability to convince others to adopt a point of view or to act in a certain way—can acquire the skills to work in sales, the law, journalism, or even politics. In effect, they can act to become a player in a new league where they have more opportunity and security.

A STATE OF MIND

The Career Activist Republic is not a political organization or an organized labor movement. It is an assembly as the Founding Fathers intended. And, like other assemblies—the Green Nation and the Red Sox Nation, for example—its membership is voluntary and shares a common outlook and sometimes, even a common vocabulary—just listen to the way Red Sox fans describe players for the New York Yankees.

Unlike those assemblies, however, the Career Activist Republic isn't driven by what people want to be. It is energized by who they are. It is an assembly of people devoted to expressing and experiencing their essential selves. Their talent.

The Career Activist Republic is a state of mind. Career activists may be proactive and energetic people in the world of work, but their community is being built with an outlook—a way of seeing themselves and their career. It is based on a belief in the potential and potency of their inherent capability—their talent—and a determination to apply that gift in whatever profession, craft or trade they may select. They see the workplace not as a cage which locks them into a static and spiritless career, but as a dynamic environment where they can (and must) chart their own course toward goals which are meaningful and rewarding for them.

Career activists don't take an oath or sign a piece of paper to confirm their citizenship in their Republic. They take a far braver step. They give themselves permission to believe in their own independence—they will not permit others to determine the course of their career—and in the sanctity of the capability with which they were endowed—they will not allow their talent to be ignored or debased. Career activists are, in short, proactive visionaries of the best they can be, the best they intend to be, and the best they are.

AN ECONOMY OF TALENT, BY TALENT AND WITH TALENT

Career activism may be a state of mind, but it creates a very tangible reality. It establishes a new and historic structure for the American workplace. The rise of career activism ends the nation's 20th Century flirtation with contracts and collective bargaining and returns it to the legitimate source of its prosperity—its citizens' heritage of individual responsibility and initiative. America was and is the home of independent, self-reliant people, not the land of union rules and card-carrying members.

The Career Activist Republic replaces America's industrial era labor mentality with a modern marketplace—a 21st Century phenomenon—an economy of talent, by talent and with talent. Its citizens can never be underbid by cheap labor overseas. They can never be overwhelmed by automation. They are impregnable because they live in the one country on earth where their talent is nurtured by the talent of all the world's people. Their talent is unmatched because their republic is unlimited. It is open to everyone.

This newest of democracies reaffirms the United States of America as the world's leader. It establishes this position, however, not with the might of its military force, but with the creativity, innovation and intellect of its workforce. A strong military will always be essential to the security of a free people, but in today's turbulent global marketplace, the quality and durability of their standard of living depends upon an economy of talent.

The Career Activist Republic realizes the power and promise of such an economy. In effect, it creates a new currency for the United States of America. The country took itself off the gold standard in 1971. The dollar hasn't been backed by anything precious since then. As one pundit put it, the greenback has become an "IOU nothing."

The Career Activist Republic corrects that decline in worth. It revalues the dollar by putting it on the talent standard. It's not yet convertible everywhere—the Republic, itself, is only now just emerging—but increasingly, America's creditors recognize that the dollar is backed by a resource even more valuable than gold or silver. It is backed by the talent of a free and talented people.

CHAPTER 7
The Ethos of a Career Activist

What makes a career activist?

What distinguishes such a person from other working men and women? And just as important, how is the way a career activist manages their own work experience in the 21st Century different from the way that employers managed the careers of their employees in the 20th Century?

FOUR CULTURAL VALUES

A career activist both performs on-the-job and directs their career in keeping with four defining values. These values form the ethos—the culture—of career activism, one that acknowledges and leverages the realities of the modern American workplace. They are not simply a reassembled set of old values, but rather an entirely new way of looking at the purpose of and possibilities in a person's work and employment.

The cultural values of career activism encompass:

1.	A new strategic imperative
2.	A new definition of loyalty
3.	A new ethical standard
4.	A new career clock.

1. A NEW STRATEGIC IMPERATIVE

For many American workers, the 20th Century solution to managing their own career was collective action. Their strategic imperative was to achieve and maintain job security. Raised with the distinctive individualism and self-reliance of the American culture, they were fully prepared for career activism. They turned, instead, to the groupism and dependence that characterized membership in the two oppositional factions of American business. They either joined a union and relied on collective bargaining to protect their careers or they joined a corporate tribe and looked to their employer for continued employment.

Whether they wore blue collars or white collars or no collar at all, millions of Americans thought union membership was the best way to reach for and grab hold of the American Dream. Office workers in the federal government, house painters in Georgia, sanitation workers in Los Angeles, automotive workers in Detroit, and teachers in New York City all decided that union regulations and rules would give them a career they could count on and an employment experience that was fair and reasonable.

Similarly, millions of other Americans chose to become a corporate man or, later in the century, a corporate woman. They sought employment with IBM and General Motors, with Wells Fargo and AT&T and proudly wore their logos on baseball hats and sweaters. Without once wincing at the term, they bought athletic gear that proclaimed they were "The Property of" this company or that. And in one key respect, at least, that statement was true. Their employers oversaw the direction, pace and ultimate apex of their careers. No matter what they did or how they did it, it was the company's financial interests which determined their employment experience.

Career activists, in contrast, believe groupism and dependence haven't worked and won't. They look at the inability of unions to preserve jobs and the propensity of employers to cut them, and conclude there is a better way. They are convinced that successful career management in the 21st Century is best achieved by going back to their American roots, by returning to core American values. For a career activist, the path to self-preservation and prosperity isn't plural action; it's individual action. And the strategic imperative isn't job security; it's "career security."

The Quest for Career Security

Career activists reject the notion that a union or a corporation or any other employer can take care of a person's career for them. However well meaning those external entities may be, they lack a detailed knowledge of each individual's aspirations and evolving capabilities at work. And without that insight, they simply cannot do what's best for each person. In the case of a union, that means they devolve to the fatal common denominator in a modern economy and do what's best for the average person in the group. And in the case of an employer, they have, as Milton Friedman confirmed, a higher obligation to serve their shareholders, so they do what's best for the company's bottom line.

Given those realities, career activists believe that only the individual, him or herself, can do what's best for them. Only they have the intimate knowledge of their own talent and how they would be best served using it in the world of work. Only they have the undivided and unflinching commitment to their own version of the American Dream and to the kind of employment that will advance them toward its achievement.

Managing one's own career, therefore, is an act of self-respect—a declaration of a person's right to meaningful and rewarding work. It is also, however, their acknowledgement of an important responsibility. Career activists take charge of their careers because they believe that such personal involvement is the way the rights of full equality in the workplace are earned. And as with other aspects of American citizenship, that responsibility is nontransferable. It cannot be outsourced to a union, to an employer, to a boss or mentor, or to one's parents or business contacts. Career self-management is something only the individual can do, and they must, if they expect to achieve career security.

That form of security creates a new defensive posture for career activists. It empowers them to practice martial arts in their career. They can safeguard their future without having to depend upon an outside agent. They are able to tackle workplace challenges and deflect economic jolts on their own. They can employ the force of their own inherent capability to protect themselves. And, they don't have to be Jackie Chan to do so.

The job security promised by unions and employers was always a hollow form of protection. Unions demanded it and employers offered it when times were good—when security wasn't needed— and abandoned or denied it when times were bad—when employees were desperate to have it. It may have been codified in union contracts or promised by employers, but workers relied on it at their own peril. Nobody expected a job for life, but they did expect 10 years or 20 years of loyal service with an organization to count for something. The Great Recession proved it didn't.

Career security, in contrast, is a much more realistic form of protection. It does not guarantee that a person will always be employed in any one job or for any one employer. Career security does, however, provide them with an employment guarantee. And, that guarantee is both durable and dependable. It ensures that a person will always be able to find work and to do so in a job of their choosing.

While job security is a "benefit" unions can only negotiate and only employers can offer; career security is a state of being that the individual creates for him or herself. They don't have to rely on the bargaining skills of some union lawyer or the quality of leadership in the organization for which they work. They depend, instead, on themselves to direct their career toward experiences and goals that will reinforce and extend their talent. And, it is that well-honed capability—their own capacity for excellence—which protects them in the workplace. They are so good at what they do that anything bad can be overcome or avoided altogether.

The Collegiality of Career Activism

While career security cannot be created by turning one's career over to a union or corporate tribe, it is diminished by the other extreme of behavior—by individual isolationism and anti-social practices. Hence, one of the dominant traits of career activists is their collegiality. They seek out, enjoy and benefit from interaction with their peers. They want the collegiality of groupism without its downsides.

Today, that interaction typically occurs in two kinds of collaborative assemblies:

• Social media sites on the Internet

and

• Professional associations and societies.

While the Internet has, almost since its inception, provided venues such as newsgroups and job board forums to facilitate group discussions online, it is social media sites that have captured the attention and participation of the public at large. Technically, these sites include their precursors as well as blogs, wikis and even photo-sharing sites, but to most working people, they are places that enable them to make contacts and network.

For job seekers, social media sites open the door to more employment opportunities. For recruiters, they offer access to more of the candidate pool. And for everyone else, they are a kind of virtual watercooler where work-related information and gossip can be shared with others. They include such sites as LinkedIn.com, Ryze.com, Xing.com and Ziggs.com. And since the Great Recession, their popularity has grown dramatically.

LinkedIn.com, for example, had 10 million members worldwide in 2007. In early 2010, that figure had grown six-fold to 60 million members. In other words, during that single three-year stretch, the site was adding the equivalent of the population of Philadelphia to its membership rolls every single month.

Despite this phenomenal popularity, however, social media sites are not a viable alternative to groupism. They do not provide the full dimensions of collegiality required for career security. They support networking—although even that is seldom performed on social media sites in a way that forges effective professional relationships— but not the occupational growth and development that is a core tenet of career activism. They enable people to connect and communicate with one another, but not to expand or even replenish their capacity for excellence. In short, social media sites contribute to a person's career security, but the contribution is modest at best.

For a more fulsome kind of collegiality, career activists turn to professional associations and societies. According to the American Society of Association Executives, there are now 86,054 trade and professional associations in the United States. That's one association for every 1600 or so American workers. Collectively, these organizations encompass virtually every profession, craft and trade, from AARP (the American Association of Retired Persons) and the American Institute of Certified Public Accountants to the American Welding Society and the American Society of Travel Agents.

Although all associations tailor the resources they provide to the needs of their members, most offer:

- professional networking in online forums or communities and more traditional venues such as conferences and meetings;

- education and training in subjects deemed essential to occupational expertise;

- certification that attests to the level of knowledge attained in a profession, craft or trade;

- research and publications to expand and refine individual growth and development; and

- access to local chapters or affiliates where peers in a given community can meet face-to-face and get to know one another.

Career activists practice collegiality because they know it helps them to achieve the excellence that undergirds career security. They may participate in one or more social media sites—doing so is free, after all—but they throttle their involvement with limited expectations. For the sustained protection of their career, most rely on the services and support of their professional association or society. They relish that collegiality and the independence it promotes. They do not turn the direction of their careers over to those groups, however, but instead leverage their resources to set their own course, one that best secures the future they want.

2. A NEW DEFINITION OF LOYALTY

Traditionally, America's workers have been conditioned to believe that the workday belonged to their employer, and the rest of the day belonged to them. In practice, however, those two periods of time were never accorded equal priority.

Employers have long acted as if they purchase the talent of their employees—some even call their recruiters their "talent acquisition teams"—and that their ownership takes precedence over everything else. It gives them the right to intrude into not only the rest of a worker's day, but also into the rest of a worker's life. Their paycheck doesn't buy just a 40 or 50 or 80 hour workweek, it acquires their workers' holidays, vacation time and sick days, as well.

This lopsided arrangement was bad enough, but what was worse was that it became the definition of loyalty in the American workplace. If an employee felt abused by such treatment—if they left their employer for what they hoped would be a better work situation—they were branded a traitor. And, if they got to their new employer, found the same corrosive behavior and left for yet another organization, they were stigmatized as a "job hopper."

Employers, on the other hand, could lay off workers by the thousands and count on the Wall Street crowd to applaud their move as smart management. They could promise job security and describe their employees as assets, but if they reneged on their commitments and treated their workers as liabilities, they would be lionized by business school professors and the investment gurus on late night television.

Loyalty, at least as it has come to be practiced in many places in the American business community, is a one-way street. It serves the interests of employers by demanding the unflagging, come-what-may commitment of workers, but it leaves those same workers without any reciprocal level of support. Employees are expected to be loyal to the organization that pays them, but the organization is under no similar obligation to be loyal to its employees in return.

A New Two-Way Form of Loyalty

Career activists reject this inequality of loyalty. They believe they have as much right to their workday and to their wellbeing as employers have to theirs. Even more radical is their notion that a paycheck does not commit them to even eight hours of labor per day, designed solely to address the wants and needs of their employers. Career activists see their work, instead, as an investment in what serves their own best interests. They will spend countless hours on that task—on earning the deep and enduring satisfaction that comes from doing their best work—but not one minute on ensuring the quarterly earnings of some corporation.

Career activists thus violate a cardinal rule of American business. Fareed Zakaria, the author of *The Post-American World*, puts it this way: "... if you are trying to do something that is genuine and lasting, actually don't do the thing that every marketing slogan and every business school will tell you: Listen to your customer." For working men and women, those customers are their employers. And as Zacharia advised, when employers begin to bluster with endless and all-consuming demands, career activists look them in the eyes and stick their fingers in their ears.

Career activists, then, are uppity employees. They refuse to be any employer's property. To these persons of talent, organizations are simply the transient users of their talent, and that talent is only on loan to them and only for as long as it serves their own best interests. In other words, the owners of talent are those in whom it is endowed. Each individual person is the rightful owner of their personal capacity for excellence. And, it is that person to whom a career activist listens. They pay attention to themselves.

Ironically, this seemingly self-interested approach to employment actually equalizes the benefits of loyalty. When a career activist does their best work, they also serve the best interests of their employer. They may be doing it for themselves, but the outcome of their effort provides a full and sufficient return on an employer's investment in them. By being loyal to themselves—by ascribing as much importance to their own wellbeing as employers ascribe to theirs—they are being loyal, as well, to the organizations that depend upon their talent.

This balance of benefit is the new dynamic in loyalty. It establishes the right of a person to work for him or herself even as they are employed by a for-profit company, a not-for-profit organization, an educational institution or even by their local, state or the federal government. It replaces the "you're ours until we toss you out the door" credo of employer-centric loyalty with the "what's ours is yours as long as we both benefit" outlook of career activists. And, that assertion of their personal equality in the workplace liberates them. It is their Emancipation Proclamation.

The Quid Pro Quo of Two-Way Loyalty

Despite its obvious benefits, some workers may be troubled by this alternative concept of loyalty, at least initially. They have been conditioned for so long to accept the preeminence of their employer's wellbeing that they feel guilty giving equal weight to their own. That unease is further compounded by the insistence of career activists that their interests are actually the first among equals—the health of their career is more important (to them) than the financial fettle of their employers.

For some, that view seems almost blasphemous. It isn't just disloyal; it is treason and worse. The royal stature of corporations has been so engrained in American culture that rejecting it feels almost like a transgression, like a violation of the laws of nature.

The Founding Fathers, however, taught Americans otherwise. They declared that all people are free, and that their freedom cannot be abridged by monarchs or masters of the universe or petty princes of this corporation or that. In the world of work, free working men and women are not required nor should they be asked to swear fealty to their employers. They may be loyal to them, but that loyalty is freely given and, just as freely, can be taken away.

This right to self-determination is a hallowed tenet of American citizenship. As with all inalienable rights, however, it is guaranteed, but not provided. It is not an entitlement, but must, instead, be earned. Workplace freedom requires a payment in deeds, in action.

This quid pro quo of citizenship is not always recognized by busy Americans. A 2009 poll conducted by *Time* magazine, for example, suggests that many in the population want to eat their cake without first having to bake it. Over two-thirds of the respondents—68 percent—said that their fellow Americans "do not live up to their responsibilities as citizens." They are practitioners of fast food citizenship. They don't have time for the preparation or participation required for a healthy society.

Such indifference, however, is more a reflection of the times than it is a statement about the country's commitment to its citizenship responsibilities. For better or worse, Americans step up to their obligations in times of need—when what they hold dear is attacked or threatened—and let those obligations slide when the risk to those cherished possessions seems low. Immediately after the terrorists struck on 9/11, the vast majority of Americans were active citizens determined to protect their democracy. Years later, with no subsequent attack of any magnitude on the homeland, the threat seems much less proximate and the "need" for citizenship less apparent.

It is a dangerous way to practice democracy, but it explains the behavior of career activists today. The threat posed to the democracy of talent by a turbulent and unpredictable global economy is now very real to them. They can see it in their lives and in the lives of those they care about. It surrounds and engulfs them, and it is already exacting terrible consequences. That proximate danger is dissolving their indifference. They are becoming active citizens of the workplace because they believe that accepting such a responsibility is the only way to protect themselves and their families in the present and the future.

Career activists fulfill their responsibility by striving continuously to do their best work. They seek employment opportunities with organizations that support and encourage them to perform at their peak, and they devote the fullness of their talent to reaching and even exceeding that standard every workday. The effort they make is the essence of a new and more rational form of loyalty. Unlike the one-way street of employer-centric loyalty, it benefits both the individual and the organization. There is absolutely nothing wrong with or shameful about such a balanced outcome, and career activists are comfortable demanding and delivering it.

3. A NEW ETHICAL STANDARD

Organizations are inanimate. They are lifeless shells that are unable to do anything on their own. Organizations do not make decisions, and they do not act. And for that reason, they cannot misbehave. Only the people who lead and work for them can, and sometimes, they do.

While most Americans would acknowledge that distinction, no less an authority than the U.S. Supreme Court has obliterated it. In January of 2010, it published a ruling in which it accorded the First Amendment right to free speech to organizations. Inanimate entities, they opined, are just as entitled to raise money and voice their opinions in election campaigns as American citizens.

The ruling simply codifies an emerging conceit of artificial innocence among many in American society. They deny human culpability for mistakes and misdeeds and, instead, assign the blame to the organization where they occurred. A late 2009 news report from *The New*

York Times offers a case in point. It read:

> 66 The whistle-blower, a former Seagate employee named Paul A. Galloway, has provided what is described as 'an eyewitness account' accusing Seagate of taking hard-drive technology from Convolve and incorporating it into its own products, according to documents filed recently with a federal court in Manhattan.
>
> The court filings include claims by Mr. Galloway that Seagate, the world's largest producer of computer hard drives, tampered with evidence tied to Convolve's nearly 10-year-old patent infringement case against the company."

The organization, according to this account, was the source of the misbehavior. It and not its employees had broken the law. And, that self-insulating device has become an ethical blind spot in American culture. If the media mention people at all in their reports of unethical, illegal or just plain stupid workplace activity, they usually point their finger at corporate leaders.

Those leaders, of course, are ultimately responsible for all of the actions that occurred on their watch. In most cases, however, they are not the ones who actually performed the deeds. They may have permitted, encouraged or even ordered that something be done, but they are not the ones who did it. They are accountable, but nothing at all would have happened if someone else—an employee—hadn't agreed to go along.

Similarly, even the largest and most powerful organizations cannot execute a plan or implement a policy on their own. It doesn't matter whether they are established with articles of incorporation or statutory documents; it's irrelevant how they are described by the lines and arrows on a chart; and it's of no importance whether they possess registered trademarks or legally protected brand names. Organizations require people to act on their behalf. They need workers to do their bidding. And all too often, those workers have acted as henchmen and performed misdeeds that, large or small, hurt everyone.

Even worse, American workers have often set the bar low on their own. For example, according to an analysis by the Missouri Small Business & Technology Centers, employee theft in the U.S. now costs $40 billion a year. Their employers aren't doing the stealing, however; the workers are. And, the harm that results is pervasive. With the current median income in the U.S. at just over $27,590 a year, that theft—if it didn't happen—would put almost 1,500,000 people back to work. Moreover, that's just the cost of what gets discovered. It's estimated that 75 percent of the theft that occurs in the workplace isn't even uncovered!

Holding Themselves to a Higher Standard

Career activists acknowledge the role of people in setting workplace values and culture. It is the foundation for their acceptance of a new ethical standard—one that obligates them to distinguish between right and wrong actions in their work. American soldiers are expected to exercise such discretion in the heat of combat—when the calculus determines life or death—so career activists believe it is neither unrealistic nor asking too much to expect working men and women to do the same on-the-job. If the American people can demand that those who defend them do so in accordance with the Geneva Convention and the rules of war, then they should hold themselves to a similarly strict set of rules in their workplace behavior.

As one U.S. Army Captain put it to a village's elders in Afghanistan, "You know, from our past, that my Soldiers will put themselves in harm's way before endangering your lives, because that is our responsibility as Soldiers ...." Career activists needn't make that kind of danger laden sacrifice, of course, but they do forego any advantage or benefit they might gain by harming their employers, their customers, their coworkers or their community.

That commitment means more than simply adhering to the letter of the law. Certainly, career activists don't steal from their employers. But equally as important, they don't stoop to lying or cheating either. They are, for example, the human resource manager who refuses to backdate stock option grants for the executives in her company. They are the commissioned salesperson who will not sell a product he knows is defective. They are the engineer who refuses to approve construction work that is shoddy and dangerous even if it delays the project. And, they are the actuary who will not sign a financial statement they know to be untrue regardless of the pressure they get from their boss.

Career activists do not set themselves up as the ethics police, but they do hold themselves to a high standard of personal conduct. They refuse to stoop to behavior that they know is wrong or to justify it as something they were "forced" to do by their superior. They strive to be the principled citizens of the workplace. Career activists will not work for organizations that condone, encourage or require illegal, unethical or inappropriate behavior. And if, by chance, they find themselves employed by one, they refuse to go along.

Working to Achieve "Fairfillment"

This commitment to ethical workplace behavior is best described as "fairfillment." A career activist works for their individual fulfillment, but believes the accomplishment of that end depends upon their first embracing *fairness*.

The dictionary defines the word *fair* as "being consistent with ethics." Hence, a career activist serves their own best interests by respecting the best interests of everyone else. They will not obey an illegal directive from their boss because harming the community or the planet prevents them from being fulfilled. They will not cut corners, shade the truth or hide dangerous situations because victimizing those around them diminishes both who they are and who they aspire to be.

Career activists take such a stand knowing full well that it can have negative consequences. They may suffer the disapproval and even the public criticism of their supervisor. They might be ostracized by coworkers who are unwilling to hold themselves to a similar standard. They may see a decline in their performance evaluation and, therefore, lose a raise or promotion they would otherwise have earned. And, they might be fired because, ironically, they "don't live up to" the expectations of their employer.

There's no question that the impact of these consequences can be onerous and even damaging, especially in today's difficult economic climate. They can (temporarily) derail a person's progress in their career, undermine their financial security and impose a psychological or emotional burden on them and their family. The one thing these outcomes cannot do, however, is diminish their self-respect. Career activists are not perfect—they make the same mistakes and missteps as other people—but they always know that they have done so while reaching for the high bar of personal integrity. They may suffer setbacks along the way, but they never suffer a blow to their self-esteem.

4. A NEW CAREER CLOCK

In the 20th Century, most working men and women focused on their career just once each year—during their annual performance appraisal and salary review. That habit grew out of the relatively slow pace of change in the 20th Century workplace and the widespread belief that employers would deliver on their promises of job security. Business cycles were unsettling, but their impact—though unpleasant to experience—was never long-lasting and did not change the dynamics of employment. Even when a downturn did affect them, people could count on the world of work returning to "normal" and usually in relatively short order, so there was no need to be concerned about or even pay much attention to their career.

All of that changed with the rise of the global marketplace. Today's highly integrated and interdependent world economy has made career stability and predictability quaint historical artifacts. At any given moment, a revolutionary new product or service, a game-changing organizational structure or a breakthrough process design can emerge anywhere around the world and impact every other workplace on the planet. A development in Beijing or Copenhagen can, as a result, affect the job market in Boston or Cleveland and do so in a matter of months, not years.

Additionally, the Great Recession produced so much unemployment across so many career fields and industries that millions of American workers now labor and live in a constant state of fear. Although the economy has strengthened, its legacy of disruption is still forcing organizations to fight for their survival, and that struggle leaves even their most dedicated employees exposed and vulnerable. They come to work not knowing if they will have a job, and they go home at night terrified of what might happen while they are out of the office. They may be earning a paycheck, but it is denominated in anxiety.

A Second Job That Pays Out in Pride

The global index of uncertainty may have risen to fearsome heights, but it has not left workers helpless. The nation has not entered a modern Dark Age. Individual Americans are not now hostage to economic forces that are too big to overcome. They are not the hapless pawns of modern capitalism.

America's workers can protect themselves even in such an unstable and unpredictable environment. They will have to break some old habits, they will also have to learn some new behaviors, but their careers can be made more resilient and better able to withstand the ferment in the today's and tomorrow's workplace. Their future—no matter how hopeless it may seem at any given moment—can be recast to offer genuine promise and even prosperity.

Career activists commit themselves to achieving that new vista of American opportunity. In order to do so, however, they must reset their career clock. Instead of attending to their career once a year, they focus on it every day. They counteract the lack of occupational nutrition in the workplace by engaging in a daily supplement of career strengthening behavior. They constantly monitor the status of their career and do whatever they must to preserve and protect its health—day-in, day-out; week-in, week-out; month-in, month-out.

In effect, career activists take a second job, one that pays out in pride. It is not a part-time or weekend appendix to their primary occupation, but a full time and essential role to which they devote the full measure of their talent. Every day, career activists make their best effort to contribute to their employer's success and to work for the continuous realization of their own success. The former provides a measure of protection in a hostile environment, while the latter advances their personal interests in an economy freshening with opportunities, Together, they create the ideal state for a working person in America's modern economy.

Career activists know that their employers have changed the rules of the game, so they've responded by changing the game itself. They've gone from playing football, where they focus exclusively on a single role—either offense or defense—to playing basketball, where they do both. They work in a way that reinforces their security in the present and increases their access to security in the future.

Activism Isn't Workaholism

As trying as taking on an additional role may at first sound, a career activist's workday isn't any longer than those of others in the workforce. Career activists aren't workaholics. They don't spend 18 hours a day or seven days a week on-the-job. They enjoy their life outside the workplace as well as within it by being very focused and disciplined in how they work.

A career activist doesn't have the time to be checking Facebook on their office computer or to be engaging in gossip sessions around the company watercooler. They chat with friends or call their spouse during breaks in their work, but those breaks are brief and carefully controlled. They are committed to delivering a full and appropriate return on their employer's investment in them and to making a full and appropriate personal investment in their own career. And, to accomplish that double entendre of work, they know they have no time to waste. They must be both productive on-the-job and dedicated to realizing their fullest potential in their field of work.

Career activists accept this more rigorous day because it alone provides the one thing they cannot live without. What drives them, however, is very different from what motivates the nation's economic bubble-makers. They don't spend 18 hours a day or 7 days a week on-the-job in order to earn a high six figure or, better yet, a seven figure income. They don't grab every possible hour of overtime or labor away on a second shift just to live in a McMansion or drive a tony car. Career activists are no less hard working than the richest Americans, but they work for a more enduring form of wealth. They work for personal pride.

Career activists are people of talent who refuse to accept second class status on-the-job. Every day, they work to keep their occupational capability so strong that no employer would dare treat them as 3/5 of a person. Every day, they devote themselves to making an on-the-job contribution so valuable that no employer would risk denying them their inalienable rights in the workplace. Career activists respect themselves too much to surrender or forsake the hopefulness of every moment they have in the American workplace. And every moment they have outside it, as well.

The new career clock of career activists not only measures a more determined beat in their careers, however, it also signals a new era has begun for America's working men and women. This moment—this rich instant in the passage of history—is their time. A time to fulfill their destiny. A time to reinstate their rights in the American workplace, not by collective action or corporate tribalism, but by dint of hard work and the excellence inherent in their talent.

CHAPTER 8

People of Talent

Historically, talent has been viewed as a select capability possessed by a select few. It is the extraordinary skill or aptitude of extraordinary people. Most Americans know about the talent of Meryl Streep, Muhammad Ali, Stephen King and Taylor Swift. But, the notion that only they have talent is a misperception, especially in the United States. In this country, talent is actually a very democratic ideal.

THE EQUALITY OF TALENT

As every school child in America learns, the Declaration of Independence holds that "all men are created equal." Today, that phrase is interpreted to include all people, regardless of their age, gender, ethnicity, religion or national origin. They may be very different from one another or live their lives in very different ways, but every American citizen has the same inherent worth and dignity.

This belief in and commitment to equality among individuals obliges Americans to recognize the presence of talent in every person. Including themselves. In essence, each American is, by their very nature, a person of talent. All Americans are endowed with the gift of a special capability or aptitude—special not because it's rare, but because it enables them to be special—to excel.

And, because of that undifferentiated access to excellence, the talent of one person is unquestionably no better than the talent of another. There are differences in talent, to be sure, but those differences do not make one kind of talent better than another. Excellence has no rankings. Therefore, just as all Americans have an identical right to Life, Liberty and the pursuit of Happiness, they all have an identical claim to talent and to being the exceptional person it empowers them to be.

THE PERVERSE EFFECT OF WOW! TALENT

Despite its roots in America's founding documents, the equality of talent is widely denied. From kindergarten on, for example, Americans are subjected to the notion of a "normal distribution" or bell-shaped curve in their academic performance. From their most formative stages of development, they learn that only a precious few individuals can excel, an equal number of misfortunes will fail, and the rest of any classroom is fated to inhabit the average middle ground. In short, the nation's educational system teaches the majority of students that they are unequal to their smarter peers and that such a judgment is "normal."

The notion of a normal distribution, however, was developed to describe the behavior of data, not people. There is no proof at all that it applies to academic ability or intelligence quotient (IQ) scores, let alone talent. What began in the 18th Century as a mathematical formulation to explain the roll of dice was bastardized in the 20th Century by educators who meant no harm, but left generations of American students unsure of their ability to contribute to society.

And yet, the expression of talent does often seem very unequal. Americans have no trouble identifying the talent of Shaun White, whose maneuvers on a snow board have won him two Olympic gold medals. They find it more difficult to see talent in a long and unbroken record of safe driving by a city bus driver. Similarly, they can ooh and ahh at the creations of a Julia Child, but they take for granted the satisfying breakfast they get from a cook in the local coffee shop.

This perception of inequality is not based on the nature of the people involved, but on the tasks to which their talent is applied. Although we tend to exalt those whose talent we recognize, it is their deeds that impress us. Indeed, many people think that for an act to be an expression of talent, it must be able to make us exclaim in awe or, at least, warrant a ribbon. Talent isn't talent, in this view, unless it draws a Wow!.

The search engine Yahoo!, for example, asked visitors to its site to list the kinds of activity that require a display of talent. Almost all of the submissions were similar to this one:

1.	Music
2.	Stand-up comics
3.	Sports
4.	Art (drawing)
5.	Acting

And this interesting variation on the same theme:

1.	Voice/singing ability
2.	Flexibilities/double joints etc.
3.	Academic/born with a stellar memory
4.	Acting ability
5.	Knowing how to play an instrument without instruction
6.	Sixth scense [or more likely "sense"]

95

As these responses make clear, people are simply more conscious of and impressed with the expression of talent in creative, intellectual and athletic endeavors than they are in the hum drum woof and wane of ordinary lives. They may work successfully for 30 years as a professional salesperson or be the person everybody else turns to when a computer breaks down, but they do not equate their work to that of a professional ball player or an actor in film. It's just easier to recognize and appreciate talent when it involves rare or out-of-the-ordinary activity. Such acts stand out and that differentiation, they assume, is itself proof of something exceptional—of talent.

This selective assignment of talent, however, has a terrible consequence. It causes countless Americans to believe that those who do out-of-the-ordinary things—the people who can Wow a crowd—are themselves extraordinary. These individuals are both different and better than everyone else.

Most people, of course, never race in the Olympics or turn in an Academy Award winning performance. They work in "ordinary" occupations. They perform "commonplace" tasks. And, consciously or unconsciously, that lack of distinction causes them to see themselves as an average person. Worse, that self-assigned insignificance causes them to accept a state of personal inequality. At least when it comes to talent, they believe, they are second-rate and thus inferior.

The impact of that self-diminishment is bad enough on a person's ego, but even more perverse, it undermines their drive to realize their own excellence. Since they are inferior, they have no chance of equaling the feats of others. So, they tell themselves, why bother. They let the brass ring pass by. In effect, they give up on themselves.

THE GIFT OF GARDEN VARIETY TALENT

Thankfully, this modern perversion of talent does not change human nature. Despite the misperceptions, talent—the capacity for excellence—exists in all people. And because that is so, the talent used to perform uncommon feats is no different from the talent used to perform even the most mundane deeds exceptionally well. Celebrated talent is no better than "garden variety" talent that is expressed quietly and without breathless color commentary or thunderous applause.

Both kinds of talent have value. One has market value that is denominated in fortune—just look at what LeBron James is paid—and in fame—no one would miss Lady GaGa on the street. The other has intrinsic value that is denominated in fulfillment—the self-realization that is achieved through the perfection of a person's endowed capability—and in pride—the satisfaction that comes from doing one's best in a meaningful endeavor.

Those two expressions of talent, however, share the same root. They both begin as unopened gifts. Both can be used or not at the discretion of their owner. And, they both can be employed to their peak or not, depending on the degree to which they are nurtured and managed. Talent is what a person is naturally good at, but it does not yield excellence by itself.

Indeed, it's not what a person's talent is, but what they do with it that matters. What distinguishes the talented person is not that they are an author or singer, but that they are the best author or singer or the best accountant or pharmacist or best anything else they can be. They work tirelessly at perfecting their talent because, unlike wisdom, talent does not mature with age. Talent may be an inherent capability, but it is an unfinished one. So, it is up to each individual to identify their talent and, equally as important, to develop and use it effectively during their life's work.

When people accept that responsibility, they dignify all work and their own work, in particular. The manifestations of talent are as diverse as humankind, so every occupation—even the grittiest and lowest in prestige—is worthy of respect if it enables people to practice their talent. And, every person earns self-respect by opening up their talent to the fresh air of expression in their career.

There are, of course, many different ways to achieve that expression. The single best way, however, is in an occupation which enables a person to test their talent in challenges that are meaningful and worthwhile to them. The daily quest to perform at their peak— to push up to and, if possible, extend the boundaries of their own excellence—is the straightest path to the perfection of their talent. And, it is the realization of that state which provides the intense sense of fulfillment and pride that comes from living their life at work to its fullest. From expressing and experiencing the epitome of themselves.

THE DISRESPECT OF DISMISSED TALENT

For years, career counselors and coaches have been urging those in the workforce to find their talent and put it to work. Don't earn a living, they urge; make a life. As most people learn early on, however, it's a task that's not easily executed and all too easily put off.

Many people, for example, educate themselves or acquire significant expertise in a particular occupation, but that occupation, sadly, is totally unrelated to their talent. They can earn a PhD in mechanical engineering, yet have a talent for building interpersonal relationships. Or, they come out of college and launch right off on a career where they acquire genuine expertise, but never use their talent. They may work for 15 years in human resource management and, in the process, acquire a deep knowledge of that field, yet their talent may actually be mechanical intuition, the gift of understanding how machines work.

In other instances, a person may know precisely what their talent is, but be content to ignore it. They may know that they have a gift for teaching, yet pursue investment banking because it offers much higher compensation. Or, they may excel at playing the guitar, but pursue a career in real estate because they or their spouse or their parents or their friends don't consider music a legitimate or serious occupation.

Sadly, the American workforce has many individuals who fall into one of two groups: they are either accomplished in a career field that does not allow them to use their talent or they are so indifferent to their talent that they never even bother to express it. As dissimilar as these groups are, however, they have one key aspect in common. They both disrespect themselves. Somehow, they have come to believe they are not good enough or worthy enough to be a person of talent. They think so little of themselves that they—of their own free will—deny their right to one of the human species' unique and most wondrous attributes.

Career activists, in contrast, celebrate this gift. To them, their talent is an heirloom of humanity. It is a precious resource, and they have been entrusted with its safekeeping.

To meet that responsibility, they must use their talent during their passage in life—it is deserving of recognition and they are deserving of the fulfillment and pride it provides. No less important, they must also leave their talent better than it was when they began. They must reinforce and expand it even as they draw on and apply it. And, that end can only be achieved, career activists believe, by investing the time and effort necessary to achieve both:

- self-knowledge

and

- self-expression.

MEETING THE PERSON A PERSON WAS MEANT TO BE

Career activists give themselves permission to explore their heart and mind for their talent, and they spare no effort in doing so. They are determined to discover the gift with which they have been endowed. Achieving that self-knowledge, however, can be especially difficult in the culture of modern America.

Well meaning parents, counselors and teachers press young adults to acquire the skills they'll need to earn a living before they have acquired the knowledge of who they are and what they most like to do. They are pushed to be successful before they have a chance to figure out how to be satisfied. And fulfilled. So, not surprisingly, many aren't.

One poll found that almost nine-out-of-ten American workers (88 percent) are discontent. They are citizens of the freest nation on earth, yet feel imprisoned by a job that does nothing for them. They spend their days, therefore, daydreaming about what it would be like to do something else—something interesting and worthwhile.

Career activists push back at this national compulsion to leap before you look. They are determined to get to know themselves and, through that intimate awareness, to discover their talent.

For some, this self-knowledge will come in trade school or college, while others must wait until they are engaged in the world of work. The first group includes individuals who have a talent that aligns with the departments of study in academia; they are perpetual learners in the best way to use their talent. The second and far larger group represents those who must try on various occupations in the

100

workplace to find the one that fits them best; they are serial searchers for the most rewarding applications of their talent.

There's no right or wrong way to acquire this knowledge of oneself, but however it's accomplished, career activists do not stop until they meet the person they were meant to be. And, once they have been introduced, they refuse to be separated from them. They want that person in all of their life, but especially in the one-third of it they will spend at work.

TAKING THE ME OUT OF MEDIOCRITY

Career activists also believe that the overriding purpose of employment is to express and experience their talent. To be able to work according to such a standard, however, they must first dedicate themselves to expanding and then to refining their knowledge of the field in which it will be used. The perfection of talent requires both of those developments—the extension of a person's inherent capability to its broadest possible range in their chosen occupation and the enrichment of that capability to its greatest possible depth in that field.

Those developments do not occur and then end. They are not complete when a person graduates from college or when they receive an AARP membership card. They are perpetual endeavors, and they must take place in the classroom and on-the-job. They require formal education and training and real world experience. Both are essential—they are the food and water of talent—yet some people limit their effort to acquiring one or the other.

There are those who acquire the knowledge for self-expression—they know what to do with their talent at work—but use as little of it as possible on-the-job. They are book rich and job poor. Others acquire the experience necessary to use their talent effectively at work—they know how to apply their talent on-the-job—but they let their talent degrade into obsolescence. They are work savvy and occupation deficient.

These self-diminished individuals aren't confined to any one cohort of the workforce. They are found in all three of contemporary America's generations. They are Baby Boomers, Gen Xs, and Millennials. Though different in many other ways, they are exactly alike with respect to their limited expression of excellence. By debasing their talent, they become card-carrying members of the "mediocrity nation." They are content to do just enough to get by.

Their complacency is apparent to everyone but themselves. It was aptly captured in a 2008 cartoon by NGenius. The first frame shows a man asking his supervisor, "Boss, when is my salary increase effective?". The supervisor replies, "The same day you become effective.". So, what does the man do? In the second and final frame of the cartoon, he unburdens himself to a coworker by declaring, with utter cluelessness, "My request for a salary increase was just denied.".

Career activists refuse to fall into this addiction to mediocrity. They know they have the inherent capacity to be a champion at work—a master in their field—and they are determined to be that person. They seek to express their gift by working at tasks that are meaningful and satisfying to them. They want to experience what it's like to be the best they can be. And, they understand that the only way to accomplish those goals is to perfect their talent.

THE LAWS OF TALENT

Achieving self-knowledge and self-expression demands that career activists continuously test the limits of their talent. It obligates them to stretch its dimensions, reaching for peaks of performance they believe they can achieve and for still higher peaks they have not even imagined. Putting their talent to work depends upon their acceptance of a Deming-like quest for continuous improvement. And, that quest for self-perfection is what makes personal fulfillment and pride on-the-job possible. It is the pursuit of Happiness made real. It is the one sure pathway to the American Dream.

Though all people are equal in their ability to seek such perfection, however, all perfections are not the same. Spend fifteen minutes in the workplace, and it's undeniably clear that talent is endowed differently in different people.

For example, an individual who has a gift for persuasion may choose to apply that talent in the field of sales.

- If they devote the time and effort to perfect their talent, they will do their best work on-the-job and be fulfilled by that experience. They will be a superior performer, but their contribution may not be as great as another salesperson who is also working at their talent.

- Alternatively, this person may devote little or no time and effort to perfecting their talent, so they will never perform at their peak or be fulfilled by their work. Nevertheless, they may outdo others on-the-job, including some who are working at their talent and doing their best.

These situations illustrate the two Laws of Talent in the emerging Career Activist Republic.

The First Law of Talent

Talent may be a gift, but it takes hard self-work and dedication to recognize and experience it. That work is accomplished with discovery—the attainment of self-knowledge—and with continuous use—the daily act of self-expression.

The Second Law of Talent

Excellence is the product of conscientious self-perfection. By definition, perfection is never mediocre, but it is also never identical from one person to another. All human beings are unique in both their nature and nurturing, so their expression of perfection is always an individual accomplishment.

THE IMPERFECTION OF INDIVIDUAL PERFECTION

The two laws of talent make it clear that no matter how hard a person works to hone their capability, there is always going to be someone else who does it better. Given America's competitive culture, that reality will inevitably cause some to pose a question: if people with the same talent are not always able to perform at the same level, why bother at all to develop one's talent? If a person can't be the champion, why should they go to all the trouble to run the race?

Take Derek Jeter, the All Star shortstop for the New York Yankees, for example. He is clearly more talented than other players at his position in major league baseball. So, why should all those other shortstops make the effort to improve? If a person can never be number one, why bother to work at being number two or three or four?

The answer to this question reveals the spiritual foundation of career activism. Those shortstops who never ascend to the talent level of Derek Jeter have ascended to the major leagues. They are professional baseball players. They are excelling at what they love to do and do best. And, so too can everyone else. Maybe not in the "Bigs," but certainly as genuine "pros" in their field.

The external yardstick that places a person in an inferior position relative to someone else isn't unimportant—Americans do, after all, live and work in a competitive society—but that external measure is less important than each individual person's internal yardstick. And on that scale, they are reaching for the best they can be and, as a consequence, they are both satisfied and fulfilled.

The acceptance of this relativity of "best" is what sets a career activist apart from their peers in the workforce. They may be competing with others, but their personal measure of success—the outcome they seek to achieve—is to be the best they can be. And, if their excellence is somehow "less" than another's, they have both the humility and the self-confidence to accept the imperfection of their perfection.

But, what compels them to do so? What drives them to their own mountain top even if other mountains are taller?

Career activists know that the discovery and use of their talent—the simple, yet profound belief that they are a person of talent and can work as one—is what enables them to feel truly accomplished. And because that's so, the quest for perfection—no matter how imperfect it may be—is the one sure way they—or anyone—can experience the Happiness that accomplishment evokes. They are a career activist because they are both grateful for and determined to enhance the gift with which they have been endowed.

CHAPTER 9

The Heroism of Accomplishment

Passion is a favorite subject of many contemporary career writers. They may be more devoted to it than any other group except romance novelists. Bookstore shelves groan with such titles as *Finding Your Passion: The Easy Guide to Your Dream Career*; *Activate Your Passion, Create Your Career: No matter who you are*; and *Passion at Work: How to Find Work You Love and Live the Time of Your Life.*

Despite this literary enthusiasm, however, most working people would never put passion and work into the same sentence ... except around the water cooler where the discussion is actually about the latest office romance. They've learned the hard way that passion doesn't put food on the table or pay the bills.

WHERE HAS ALL THE PASSION GONE?

Passion is obviously important. As every great figure in every line of work has proven, it is necessary if a person is to be successful. However, it is also insufficient to ensure success.

Passion is what a person loves to do. Talent, on the other hand, is what they love to do <u>and</u> what they do well. They are infatuated with the doing of it and good enough to be employed at it. To put it another way, talent is passion put effectively to work.

Susan Boyle of Britain's Got Talent fame had a passion for singing. She sang for her church and for the occasional private gathering, but never contemplated working with her music. She didn't realize that singing was her talent, however, until she became a career activist. She didn't honor her gift until she found the courage and self-respect to compete for a chance to earn a living with her passion. And though she didn't win the contest, she accomplished her goal. She still loves her music, but now, she is employed as a professional singer.

It doesn't always turn out that way, of course. A person can be passionate about playing tennis, for example, but lack the inherent ability to be accomplished at the sport. No matter how much time and effort they devote to honing their skills on the court, they will never rise to a level of capability that enables them to compete on the professional tennis tour. They love the sport, they may even play it well, but they don't have the talent to build a career with it. Tennis can be their avocation, but not their vocation.

That undeniable fact affects legions of weekend tennis players and golfers, poker players and singers. They will never hear the roar of a huge crowd at a tourney or concert; they will never reap millions in cash prizes and appearance fees or see their photo in the tabloids at the checkout counter. They are not a public champion. They have the potential, however, to be a private one.

SAVING PRIVATE RECOGNITION

A private champion has a gift that's every bit as special as the gift of an all star or a super star. Moreover, that gift—the talent with which they are endowed—has the power to reward them in a more meaningful way. It may not shower them with celebrity or great wealth, but it will infuse them with something that is far more satisfying and enduring … if their gift is put to work.

And, that's what career activists do.

> They work with their talent, at their talent and on their talent in every job they take. Career activists give themselves permission to be who they truly are and to express and experience that person in their careers. They recognize their authentic selves—the gifted person they are meant to be—and work for them in the forty or more years they spend in the workplace. And, it's that commitment to personal integrity in their employment which produces their more meaningful reward.

What is that reward?

Unlike the ostentatious and intentionally attention-grabbing bling sported by professional athletes, a career activist's reward is an internal accolade. What honors them is not worn on a finger, hung on the wall or displayed in a trophy case. Its purpose is not to impress others or to proclaim their status as the world's winner. The reward a career activist achieves is, instead, individually and personally appreciated. It is an award of the spirit. It is Happiness.

THE UPSIDE OF DOWN

Career activists are the living embodiment of the American creed. The expression of their talent at work is "the pursuit of Happiness." It is a spiritual paycheck that is larger and longer lasting than any statuette or jewel-encrusted ring.

Of course, the cynical set in America will say that finding happiness at work is a pipe dream. It is, they will opine, a naïve, unrealistic and foolishly sentimental notion. The world of work isn't an adult version of the magic kingdom; it is, they would have people believe, an equal opportunity dungeon. And yet, social science and other research is now proving that exactly the opposite is true.

It has admittedly taken a long time to come to that conclusion. For most of its history, psychology—which describes itself as the science of mind and behavior—has dealt exclusively with the negative aspects of the human species. It has focused on people's frailties and phobias. There are 500,000 lines of text in the *Comprehensive Textbook of Psychiatry*, the bible of the field, yet just five lines are devoted to hope, one line to joy and not a single line to compassion or forgiveness or love.

This exclusive focus on people's problems finally began to shift in the late 20th Century. In 1998, for example, the Gallup Organization founded the Gallup Positive Psychology Institute. Its mission is to figure out what makes the glass half full, rather than half empty. Even before then, however, individual researchers were probing the meaning and source of happiness in humans.

THE GIFT OF GOING WITH THE FLOW

A social scientist by the name of Mihaly Csikszentmihalyi published a book in 1990 called *Flow, The Psychology of Optimal Experience*. It described interviews he had conducted with a wide cross-section of working adults. His subjects ranged from professional athletes, entertainers, and grand chess masters to those who were employed in less esoteric occupations. The goal of his investigation was at one and the same time both thoroughly mundane and sublimely extraordinary—he wanted to find out when in life people are most happy.

110

All of those who were interviewed were asked the same three questions:

- When, during the day, did they most enjoy themselves?

- What were they doing when they most enjoyed themselves?

- And, how did they feel—what was the experience like—when it happened?

The findings of this research were startling, even in the relatively benign workplace of the 20th Century. In today's leaner and meaner world of work, they seem especially improbable. Most of the people in the survey reported that:

- they most enjoyed themselves during the workday

and

- they derived their greatest pleasure—a deep and lasting happiness—when they were engaged in interesting and meaningful work.

Contrary to the mythology of America's work-for-money-to-consume-for-pleasure culture, people aren't happiest when engaged in "retail therapy" or on weekends loaded with leisure pursuits. That's not, of course, a particularly novel idea. It's a mantra practically everyone recites all the time and sadly seems to forget almost as often: *you can't buy happiness*. What Csikszent-mihalyi did was prove it.

More importantly, he discovered how happiness is actually created. It cannot be bought, but it also cannot be imagined, dreamed or thought into existence. People can't teleport themselves into happiness or create it with an avatar. Although hoping for happiness is unlikely to harm a person—and some scientists would dispute even that—it is about as effective as wishing upon a star or rubbing a rabbit's foot.

While positive thinking won't work, however, positive action will. Americans can produce happiness for themselves, and as shocking as it may seem to those laboring away in the trenches, work is the single best place to do so. Not only is suffering on-the-job not required—people don't have to endure their jobs in order to enjoy their life—they can actually be content and fulfilled there—their employment can be used to create some of their best times. They can give themselves a deep sense of satisfaction and wellbeing by simply using their gift of talent in their work.

Csikszentmihalyi surmised that this outcome occurs because "*On the job, people feel skillful and challenged, and therefore feel more happy, strong, creative, and satisfied.*" Their work, in other words, provides that rare opportunity for self-perfection which brings them to a deeper understanding of who they are and have the potential to be. It, alone, gives them a way to search for and stretch to the fullest dimensions of their talent—to achieve and experience the best they can be. That expression of their own magic leaves them profoundly fulfilled and content. And those feelings are the basic ingredients of Happiness.

THE MARATHON OF WORK

This finding doesn't mean that work should be free of arduous or exhausting endeavors. In fact, exactly the opposite is true. The optimal work—the work that produces happiness—is demanding and difficult. Its DNA is changed, however, when it employs a person's talent. They may (in fact, they should) come home from such work feeling tested and drained, but they will never head off to work that way. Their experience is positive precisely because they are pushed to do more of what they love to do and do best.

Career activists recognize this salubrious aspect of work. They select jobs that challenge them to perform at their peak. They want to be pushed to their limits so they can experience the epitome of themselves. They see employment not only as a way to earn a living, but also as a pathway for living—a physical, psychological and/or intellectual "lane"—where they can test themselves and realize more of their inherent excellence.

That kind of work creates a contest—not a race against others, but a marathon with themselves. Not up a career ladder defined by some employer, but across a career jungle gym where they determine the way forward. Not for an objective set by an organization, but to a finish line that demarks a personal victory. The resulting sense of accomplishment—the extraordinary feeling of being the best they can be—is both unique to work and the sole source of Happiness.

Csikszentmihalyi's research reveals, however, that this work-accomplishment connection is not axiomatic. In fact, it can only occur if people work in jobs that push them to use their talent as effectively as they possibly can. As he writes, "*The best moments usually occur when a person's body or mind is stretched to its limits in a voluntary effort to accomplish something difficult and worthwhile.*" In essence, the optimal experience—the time when humans feel accomplished and happy—is something that they make happen, and they do so by purposely testing themselves in tasks that are not easily performed or completed.

CHANGING THE SCALE FOR THE WORK-LIFE BALANCE

Consciously or unconsciously, career activists understand and accept what Csikszentmihalyi learned. They see the corporate Human Resource Department's focus on work-life balance as fundamentally misplaced. It implies that work is onerous, demeaning and unpleasant and thus must be balanced with the good that occurs outside the workplace. To career activists, that's backwards. They believe that people deserve a work experience that is every bit as good as the rest of their lives.

C areer activists don't give up on the one-third of their day they spend on-the-job. They expect their work to engage and challenge them, but they also accept responsibility for ensuring that it does. And, they rely on their work to find the outer most limits of their excellence, not because their employer expects it, but because they will not accept anything less from themselves. By striving for a sense of personal accomplishment, career activists know they will create a legacy that is worthy of their talent and in which they can be proud.

Does that mean career activists see their work as an endeavor that's more important than their family, their friends, their life outside the workplace? Do they really want their tombstone to read, *I wish I had spent more time in the office*.? Of course not. The human species has access to two kinds of fulfillment—happiness and joy—and both are essential to a rich and satisfying life.

Happiness is a cognitive state. It is an experience of the mind that is achieved when a person is fully engaged in a challenge that draws on their talent and enables them to reach for the apex of their excellence. As Csikszentmihalyi discovered, those challenges are most likely to occur in the workplace.

Joy, on the other hand, is an emotional state. It is an experience of the heart. Joy is achieved when we are surrounded by and fully engaged with those whom we love and who love us. And, as every person knows or comes to realize, those times are most likely to occur in their home and hometown.

THE EXTRAORDINARY COMMITMENT
OF ORDINARY PEOPLE

The Career Activist Republic respects this duality. It acknowledges the importance of joy, but also accords equal value to an individual's happiness. It adds context to the three inalienable rights that are detailed in the American Declaration of Independence: Americans are, each and every one, endowed with the Liberty to experience both the joy of Life at their hearth and the pursuit of Happiness in their work. The wisdom of the Founding Fathers was their recognition of this symmetry in the human condition and their determination to found a nation upon it.

While these rights are ascribed to all Americans, however, they do not actually exist unless they are made real. They are simply a promise on parchment unless they are practiced in person. And that reality presents every American with an unspoken but fundamental choice—do they claim their rights by exercising them or do they let them languish by ignoring them?

Most Americans instinctively and vigorously strive to experience joy in their Life. Far fewer exert the same effort in their pursuit of Happiness. This half-step approach, however, is neither irrational nor necessarily misguided. The quest for accomplishment is a daunting endeavor. Instinctively, people know that striving to be the best they can be is not easy, even in a land of opportunity. Choosing to do so, therefore, is an extraordinary commitment.

There are at least three distinct challenges to the decision:

The First Challenge

Seeking accomplishment exposes a person to the risk of falling short. They must have the courage to stretch toward an ever more complete expression of their talent, and there is always the possibility they will overreach and not meet their goal.

Career activists manage their risk by putting themselves in a position to succeed. They choose employers and jobs that provide the right challenge with the right support for them to apply their talent most effectively.

The Second Challenge

Seeking accomplishment pushes a person outside their comfort zone. They must be brave enough to go beyond what's familiar and routine, and there is no GPS, map or set of directions to indicate the best way forward.

Career activists overcome their discomfort by redefining their work as self-perfection. They choose to look beyond conventional measures of success or failure and focus, instead, on how much they can learn about themselves and their talent.

The Third Challenge

Seeking accomplishment requires a person to acknowledge and accept their own imperfection. They must be humble enough to see themselves as a work-in-progress where their potential for improvement is never fully realized, whatever their level of expertise or experience.

Career activists avoid both over and underestimating themselves by taking pride in who they have yet to become as well as in who they already are. They are not embarrassed by their incompleteness, but rather see it as confirmation of the potential and potency of their talent.

NO HOLDING BACK: HEROISM AT WORK

While the benefits of accomplishment are undoubtedly significant, so too is the effort required to achieve them. The rewards of accomplishment may be outsized, but the risk of being found wanting is great, as well. Americans are the lucky few on this planet who have the right and the opportunity to reach for the epitome of themselves. That good fortune, however, does not reduce the difficulty of the challenge.

Career activists know full well what will be asked of them, and still they are not deterred. They recognize the enormity of their endeavor, but they will not be put off. Whether it is pushing out the frontiers of science or pushing into a new market, whether it is tackling an especially difficult problem or a critically important assignment, they do not flinch from the challenge. That effervescent spunk, however, does not diminish the courage upon which it relies.

Career activists are ordinary people pledged to do the extraordinary—to pursue Happiness. They are "normal" American citizens determined to reach the summit of their excellence through their own accomplishment at work. And, that unfettered yet unpretentious aspiration ennobles their result, whatever it may be. It raises their purpose to the level of heroism—to individual exceptionalism—in the modern American workplace.

CHAPTER 10
The Actions of Career Activism

C areer activism is the active pursuit of Happiness by people of talent.

Every human being is created with talent. It is one of the defining characteristics of the human species. And yet, many of the world's people never get the chance to experience this gift. The circumstances of their life make expressing their talent impossible.

Some face caste systems or crushing poverty. Others are held back by repressive governments or religious tyrannies, and still others must contend with inadequate education or cultural biases. The specific causes are different from society-to-society, but the outcome is always the same: individual men and women are denied the right and/or the opportunity to realize their talent.

THE CHOICE OF A LIFETIME

Americans, in contrast, are not only guaranteed the right to employ their talent, they are presented with genuine opportunities to do so. There is, however, a string attached. Each person has the freedom and (in most cases) the prospects to excel, but they must choose to do so. Americans, in effect, face a very different kind of dilemma. While the possibilities are not always what they should be, every citizen is, at least by law and tradition, eligible to express their talent in the workplace. That is their heritage. But, it is not their reality. To be made real, they must claim their heritage. They must act to make it their own.

Those who choose to do so—those who commit themselves to using their talent in the pursuit of Happiness at work—are career activists. Those who elect to disregard their talent and thus their heritage of possibilities are career pacifists.

This choice is often made unconsciously, but it is made nonetheless. Occasionally, a person is lucky and finds that they are pulled to their talent by an inner voice. Happily, this "calling" gets rid of any doubt or indecision and makes the right course apparent to them. Such individuals don't choose their course; they choose, instead, to listen and accept whatever direction they are given.

In other cases—perhaps even most cases—people fall into an occupation because it is familiar to them—it's what their mother or father did, for example. Or, they take the first job that comes along after they are graduated from college—their four-year investment having produced a degree but little understanding of their inherent capacity for excellence. In essence, they too have picked a course without having actually made a choice.

While such an approach can lead to a positive outcome, all too often it doesn't. It is the functional equivalent of playing blind man's bluff with one's future. An unconsidered choice can put someone to work doing what they love to do and do best. Much more frequently, however, it sends them off on a career they endure for 20, 30 or even 40 years only to discover—when they retire or are laid off—that they have neglected their gift and turned their back on their own excellence. And, there is no way to make up for that lost time. So-called "second act careers" do not restore the opportunities that have been neglected or the self-perfection that could have been achieved.

Nobody starts out with that intention, of course. But sadly, it is what happens. Millions of American working men and women don't pursue Happiness with their work so all that's left for them to achieve is its polar opposite. They create their own Dilbertesque cubicle of despair—an endless grind of meaningless tasks and missing challenges on-the-job. They unwittingly commit themselves to a career spent entirely as a shadow of who they have the potential to be.

The worker surveys that find otherwise simply reflect this diminution of expectations. American workers may report that they are satisfied with their work, but they are using the lowest possible standard with which to make that judgment. They are stating that they are not mistreated on-the-job and earn enough money to enjoy a modest standard of living. They are not saying that they are fulfilled by their work or that they derive any Happiness from what they accomplish by doing it.

THE CARE-LESS CAREERS OF PACIFISTS

Given their work experience, it's not surprising that career pacifists don't spend much if any time at all caring for their careers. Having made an unfortunate initial choice and reaped its consequences, it's just easier for some, at least, to give up and play ostrich. Year-in, year-out, they plod along at work, hoping for the best, fearing the worst and doing nothing about either.

Still other career pacifists are content to wear rose tinted glasses. The global economy is undergoing wrenching change, yet they blithely assume that their future will look exactly like their past, only better. Prosperity is a given; all they have to do is show up. Deep down inside, they believe that America owes them a certain standard of living, and they expect it to pay up.

Regardless of their differences in motivation, however, all career pacifists care for their career in exactly the same way. They give it the cold shoulder for eleven months and thirty days of the year. It's only on the remaining day that they bother to pull their heads out of the sand or take off the rose tinted glasses and pay attention.

On that one day, their employer first confronts them with their annual performance appraisal and then subjects them to a salary review. In effect, on this single occasion, career pacifists have no choice. They are forced to think about what they are doing at work and how well they are doing it. But as soon as that (often unpleasant) event has passed, they return to their passivity.

Such drive-by shots at career self-management have a tragic impact. They turn countless Americans into "career orphans." The passivity of these working, but care-less men and women hands their future over to an outside agent, either their employers or the stony indifference of fate. And, in doing so, they effectively cancel their claim to the American Dream.

RE-SETTING THE SNAIL'S PACE OF CHANGE

A career activist is a conscientious custodian of their career. They don't give up on their career or give it away. Unlike career pacifists, they give it their full and undivided attention. And, equally as important, they give it a full measure of their talent. They acquire the knowledge and skills of career self-management so they can use their talent to guide their employment to meaningful and rewarding work.

They do so to protect both themselves and their right to the pursuit of Happiness. They know that job security is no longer a realistic option, so they seek the more reliable, but more demanding safety of career security. They also recognize that fulfillment-by-chance is a spiritless form of employment, so they strive to select jobs that will enable them to do their best work. And, in the modern American workplace, neither of those two outcomes is easily accomplished.

The world of work isn't just in flux. It's in flux at warp speed. Work-place change is happening faster than at any other time in American history. Whole industries and career fields are morphing even as Americans watch. And, while it's impossible to miss the acid reflux caused by this disruption, it's hard to appreciate the pace at which it's occurring.

Ironically, the common garden snail can help to remove this ambiguity. According to *The World Almanac and Book of Facts*, a typical garden snail travels at the almost imperceptible speed of 0.03 miles per hour. At that rate, it would have taken a snail well over a full day—33 hours, in fact—to crawl a single mile in the year 2000.

If in 2010, the same lowly mollusk increased its speed to the pace of change during that one ten-year period—if it simply accelerated enough to keep up with what was going on in the workplace using Moore's Law (which measures the rate of technological advancement in the semiconductor industry) as its speedometer—it would cover that same mile in less than an hour—actually in just over 15 minutes! From the snail's perspective, the world around it would be whizzing by, and that's exactly how the world of work is changing for America's workers.

CARE-GIVING FOR A CAREER

Historically, there has always been plenty of time to adjust to work-place changes. Today, there isn't. The only way to survive (and prosper) in the face of rapid-fire change is to move faster than the speeding bullets. In fiction, performing such a feat would require extraterrestrial powers. In the real world of work, exactly the opposite is true. All that's needed is one's adherence to the laws of physics.

Career security is now best achieved through a variation of Newton's First Law of Motion. In today's pedal-to-the-metal workplace, only a career that is moving will continue moving. And unfortunately, the converse is also true. A career at a dead stop is dead.

A career activist ensures their uninterrupted progress by always making progress. Indeed, they engage in a cycle of career care-giving activity:

- They begin by investing the time to think through their options and select the course or courses of action that makes the most sense for them at each and every point in their career.

  Change is the new norm in the workplace, yet making a change is the one thing most people most hate to do. It pushes them into the unknown, introduces uncertainty and makes them uncomfortable.

  Change is as hard on career activists as it is on everyone else, but they take charge of the change in their career, so they don't become its victim. They continuously assess its impact on their occupational field, their employer, their industry, their job and their boss, and they determine what adjustments will be necessary to sustain the forward momentum of their career.

- Next, they make the necessary preparations to implement the course(s) of action they have selected, and then they take the appropriate steps to achieve their goal(s). They acquire the additional skills or experience, meet the necessary people and perform at the required level to effect the change that's best for them

  Successfully adjusting to change doesn't happen by serendipity or wishful thinking. It requires careful planning and dedicated follow-through. It takes every bit as much talent to accomplish as does excelling at one's job.

Career activists set clear goals for themselves and make them the first priority in their work. They invest the time and effort required to develop and execute a strategy that will move them toward the next level in their self-perfection. Special circumstances (on-the-job or at home) may force them to interrupt their progress, but they do everything they can to limit the pause and get back on course quickly.

- Finally, career activists evaluate the outcome of what they've accomplished and make corrections as necessary to ensure their ongoing progress. They don't judge the caliber of their performance, but rather assess how effective it's been in achieving their goals and how best to make it more so.

Workplace flux means that circumstances and situations are never static or even stable for very long. The right choice today can be overtaken by events tomorrow, creating a new right choice for the day after that.

Career activists, therefore, pursue Happiness by converging on it. They don't set a single goal they have to hit as some penultimate bulls-eye in order to be successful. Instead, they establish a series of ever tighter bulls-eyes that successively advance them in their career.

This cycle is the perpetual dynamic of a career activist's work experience. As soon as they complete one evolution, they start into the cycle all over again. Hence, a career activist is always in motion— always taking action—and what they do always has a clearly defined and useful purpose. It is not action for action's sake but rather, action that is explicitly intended to achieve a specific and meaningful end.

The story about two men in a desert brings the difference into stark relief. Two men meet up in the middle of the Mojave Desert. One of them is carrying an umbrella; the other is carrying a car door. The man with the car door asks the man with the umbrella why he is wandering around with an umbrella in a place where it never rains. The fellow replies that when it gets hot each day, he opens the umbrella to shade himself from the sun. Then, he asks the man with the car door why he is carrying such a heavy load in such a hot place. And, that man replies that when it gets hot, he simply rolls down the window.

The fellow with the umbrella has taken beneficial action. The course he selected would, in fact, be advantageous to him. It will improve his circumstances. The fellow with the car door, on the other hand, has also taken action, but his approach does not benefit him at all. It not only fails to improve his situation, but it is also likely to harm him.

THE SELF-MORE CARE OF CAREER ACTIVISM

Career activists act in a way that benefits their own career. They do so, however, not by serf-like devotion to the interests of their employer—they don't meekly labor away to increase that organization's profits or burnish its stature in the media. Quite the contrary, a career activist focuses exclusively on being the best they can be in the workplace. The actions they take to achieve that goal will inevitably contribute to the success of their employers, but that outcome is not their primary purpose. Their main goal is to pursue Happiness through the ever more refined expression of their talent on-the-job.

Care-giving for others is a selfless act. Care-giving for one's own career is a "self-more" act. It enhances one's ability to excel and, through the expression of that perfection on-the-job, to experience the Happiness produced by personal accomplishment. A career activist, therefore, won't settle for anything less than a work environment that engages, challenges and ultimately fulfills them. And for the same reason, they will not let any employer, boss or colleague or even any well-meaning relative or friend interfere with the development and use of their talent.

The start point in this self-more act is always self-appreciation. It precedes even self-discovery. Although they may suffer some discouragement from time-to-time, most Americans are confident and secure in their sense of themselves. They are, as the saying goes, comfortable in their own skin.

Indeed, as a nation at least, Americans have never suffered from an inferiority complex. Their folk heroes are larger than life figures like Paul Bunyan and John Henry. Their heritage is full of such outsized deeds as saving the world from totalitarianism and expanding the reach of humankind into space.

All too often, however, individual Americans do not fully appreciate the potential within them. Pull together any group of Americans and ask them to identify five extraordinary people in the U.S.A., and their list will include the famous and infamous. They will cite astronauts and generals, sports heroes and preachers, past presidents and maybe even a conman or two. Almost never, however, will they list themselves—the person inside their own skin. That person is invisible, at least to them. Greatness is a trait with which Americans naturally identify, but it is also one they often fail to claim as their own.

Career activists, in contrast, are not only convinced that they have a champion inside them, they believe they have a personal responsibility to respect and honor that person. Not with parades and ostentatious jewelry, but with the quiet, sure recognition of their own potential. They must do the hard work of self-appreciation. They must act, not for action's sake, however, but for their sake. They deserve to meet the person they were meant to be.

A REGIMEN OF SELF-IMPROVEMENT

Self-appreciation is the trigger for self-knowledge. Self-knowledge, in turn, is the foundation for self-protection. And self-perfection is achieved through self-exploration and self-expression on-the-job. Collectively, these activities comprise a personalized regimen of self-improvement. They form a virtuous circle of specific actions which will refine a person's talent and enable them to realize as much of their capacity for excellence as they can.

For example, a career activist who uses their talent to work as a computer systems analyst would accomplish self-improvement by:

- Continuously upgrading their computer systems skills and knowledge so they can perform at their peak on-the-job;

- Continuously seeking employment opportunities (either with their current employer or new ones) that challenge them to grow in capability and experience with computer systems;

- Continuously reinforcing their computer systems skills with ancillary or supporting capabilities (e.g., project management, a second language) so they can take jobs that require broader talent and higher levels of performance; and

- Devoting as much time and effort to directing their own career toward success—to setting its goals, direction and pace—as they do to making a contribution to their employer's success.

Career activists are strivers, but not in the conventional sense of that term. They don't dedicate themselves to reaching the top of some employer's career ladder, but rather, to reaching the epitome of themselves. They aren't consumed with beating out others—for a promotion, a raise or professional recognition—but instead, devote themselves to doing their best work. In short, career activists want nothing more, but also nothing less than to become the most complete person of talent they can be.

Because self-improvement only occurs with beneficial actions, however, a career activist must ensure that the actions they take result in at least one of three outcomes. They must advance:

- The development of their talent;

- The application of their talent at work; and

- The management of their talent throughout their career.

THE BENEFITS OF AMERICAN DREAMERS

Each of those three spheres of action—development, application and management—is as important as the others, so all must be addressed and accomplished if the career activist is to achieve sustained self-improvement. That commitment is undeniably demanding. There is no question that, for many and maybe even most people, it will require that they be more attentive to their work conditions, more candid in assessing their own performance, and more proactive about shaping their own career than they have ever been before.

areer activism isn't for bystanders or for the faint of heart. It is for American Dreamers. It is for Americans who refuse to give in to the cynicism of so many of the nation's current thought leaders or to the sense of victimization among so many of those in the workforce. And, it is for Americans who will not give up on the wondrous gift with which they have been endowed or surrender their inalienable right to seek its expression at work.

In today's dispirited atmosphere, this activism will undoubtedly be cast as a Quixotic endeavor. It will be ridiculed as an errand of fools and fantasy lovers. The benefits that activism—and only activism—provides, however, both refute such charges and fully justify the effort.

Those benefits are:

- **Satisfaction:** the knowledge that they have done their best work;

- **Growth:** the realization of an ever fuller measure of their talent;

- **Fulfillment:** the experience of personal excellence in meaningful work;

- **Security:** the certainty that they will always be able to find work in a job that engages their talent;

and

- **Happiness:** the sense of accomplishment derived from moving ever closer to the perfection of which they are capable.

The actions of career activism pay a higher and more enduring dividend than any stock or financial derivative. They provide stronger and more durable insurance than any term or life policy. And, they create a present day and future work reality that is what every American is meant to have and deserves.

CHAPTER 11
The Development of Talent

It would be nice to think that talent springs fully formed from the womb. It doesn't. It must be nurtured and developed. For that reason, a career activist takes a paternal view of their talent. They see it as a legacy the care of which has been entrusted to them.

Their talent is as much a part of who they are as their body, and as with that physical aspect of their being, they are responsible for its good health. It is their job to nourish and grow it. Their talent is the potential they've been given to be an extraordinary person, and only they can realize it.

REFUSING TO GIVE UP ON THEMSELVES

The realization of person's talent, of course, begins with self-awareness. Some career activists are lucky. They seem instinctively to know exactly what their talent is. They come to understand, often at a very early age, that their gift is the ability to interact comfortably with different people or a facility for disaggregating complex situations into their more manageable parts or a penchant for communicating new ideas and information in an engaging manner. Whatever it is, their self-awareness is both complete and accurate with seem-ingly little or no effort on their part.

For most people, however, such self-knowledge is acquired through a process of discovery. They make a conscious effort first to figure out their talent—their inherent capacity for excellence—and then to determine how best to put it to work. They set aside the time to get to know themselves and to learn what specific behavior they instinc-tively resort to and enjoy when all external constraints and expecta-tions are eliminated. They may, for example, find that they have been endowed with the gift of compassion and feel most comfortable putting that gift to work by tending to those who are ill. Their career should be centered, therefore, on an occupation which enables them to perform that role and to perform at their peak.

Talent is a person's passion, but it is passion reinforced with practi-cality. It is what they love to do applied to work at which they can excel. With a talent for compassion, they might pursue a career as a physician, a nurse or a home health aide. There is always a range of occupations in which a gift can be put to work, so a career activist makes it their priority to figure out which fits them best. They want both to be fulfilled by their work and proud of how they do it.

High schools and colleges support self-discovery through the aca-demic preparation they provide. Such knowledge acquisition and cognitive development are obviously essential components of person-al exploration, but they are not sufficient for its completion. Indeed, most educational institutions make little or no effort to help students find their talent or the kinds of work at which they can excel. As a consequence, that connection—if it is ever established at all—occurs in a hit-or-miss journey of serial searching.

The experience of Ray Kroc, the founder of McDonalds, provides a case in point. Kroc knew early on that he had a talent for creativity. He tried first to launch a career as a jazz pianist. He loved creat-ing music, but quickly discovered that he wasn't able to do so well enough to earn a living. So, he turned his talent to creating enter-tainment with the talent of other musicians. He took a job with a radio station, booking acts to play on the air.

When that didn't provide the satisfaction he was seeking, he put his talent aside and entered the world of business. He wandered from one job to another, first selling paper cups and then selling real estate. The work wasn't especially interesting to him, but he got good enough at it to earn a living. It paid the bills and supported his family, but it didn't satisfy or fulfill him.

Finally, he went to work for a company that made multi-mixers, machines that could produce five milkshakes at one time. And, that's when he discovered a small restaurant in California. Run by the McDonald brothers, it was growing so fast it had become one of his biggest customers. It was also the place where he could do what he loved to do and did best. He found a way to put his talent to work by creating a global business. He invented a way to apply manufacturing principles to the day-to-day operation of a hamburger stand. But more than that, he created an entirely new industry, the one the world now calls "fast food."

Career activists don't see such a journey as a string of failed attempts at success. They don't think of themselves as a "jack of all trades, master of none." Nor do they buy the notion that they should stick with a job or even an occupation just to stay employed. They refuse to be boxed in or boxed out or boxed up in their quest to realize their capacity for excellence. They will leave no stone unturned in their search for what they were meant to do because they refuse to give up on themselves.

PRACTICE REALLY DOES MAKE PERFECT

As Ray Kroc's experience makes clear, the journey to self-knowledge isn't bound by a person's age or by the number of years they've spent in the workplace. The quest to discover one's talent is as important at age 62 as it is at age 22. It can happen when someone has considerable seniority or a high standing in their field and when they are lost and uncertain about what to do next in their career.

It is a basic instinct of the human species—not coded into its DNA, but threaded into its character—that people yearn to become all of the person they have the potential to be. That drive for self-perfection and expression is what separates them from beasts of burden. No less important, it is what protects them from a career that unfolds as a dull and dreary counterpoint to the rest of their life.

Self-discovery points a person in the right direction, but it does not take them to their destination. They know what they can be, but they must stay true to that vision and complete the journey if they are to realize their extraordinary self. And sadly, those who take the first step often don't take the second.

As J.M. Barrie, the author of *Peter Pan*, once wrote, "The life of every man is a diary in which he means to write one story, and writes another." Many people never do find their capacity for excellence— their talent—but just as tragic, many of those who have made the discovery never go on to acquire the ability to excel. They are hooked on mediocrity.

This group of half-complete people never commits themselves to personal development. They leave their talent unfinished because they assume it will flourish on its own. But it won't. Talent is the capacity—the readiness—for excellence. For that perfection to be realized, it must be fully educated and continuously trained. A person's talent must be taught the principles and skills of a particular occupation so that it can be expressed and experienced in that field. It has to be shown how to excel at the work it will be asked to do.

Take Michael Jordan and Kobe Bryant, individuals whose talent is athleticism. Though they are both considered "natural athletes," their talent didn't simply walk out on the court and excel at basketball. It had to learn the game. It had to be taught its offensive and defensive movements and then, those movements had to be repeated over and over again until they became "second nature." Only then— only after they had practiced using their talent effectively on the court—could they use it to excel when it really counted, in an actual game.

For that reason, a career activist sees him or herself as a "pro-in-progress." They are simultaneously a genuine professional—whether they are a computer programmer, a customer service representative or a basketball player—and a permanent student of their field. They are the expert who never ceases reaching for their personal peak of performance on-the-job. They are the perpetual master apprentice— an individual who is always striving to be better at work today than they were yesterday and always looking for ways to be better tomorrow than they are today.

WORKING FROM THE NECK UP

Practice and performance have always been seen as the keys to athletic excellence, be it in basketball or any other sport. And, continuing education has always been accepted as a necessary requirement in such licensed fields as engineering and medicine. But, for the vast majority of Americans, the notion of being a perpetual student in their profession, craft or trade is simply outside the realm of normal behavior.

This blind spot was clearly described in a 1977 book by the educator, Ronald A. Gross. The book recounts the stories of a number of "life long learners," including a New York City resident by the name of Cornelius Hirschberg. Here's how Hirschberg described his own approach to continuous development:

> **" I am stuck in the city, that's all I have. I am stuck in business and routine and tedium. But I give up only as much as I must; for the rest, I live my life at its best, with art, music, poetry, literature, science, philosophy and thought. I shall know the keener people of the world, think the keener thoughts and taste the keener pleasures as long as I can and as much as I can."**

Tragically, Hirschberg chose to expand his knowledge in fields outside of his work—to be a perpetual student of art, music, poetry, literature, philosophy and thought—and to be employed as a drone. He segregated his quest for life long learning from the one-third of his life he spent on-the-job. He read on the subway to and from work, during his lunch break and in the evening, but for the rest of his day, he was brain dead.

Career activists don't make that mistake. Whether they are rock stars or rocket scientists, they work from the neck up. They use their heads on-the-job as well as off. They believe there is much to learn in their chosen field of work and much to be gained from doing so. It is the mind which produces Happiness at work, but it can do so only if it is nurtured and refined to its fullest potential.

For a career activist, therefore, self-development is an integral and high priority facet of their career. It encompasses four spheres of potential growth:

- Their talent—the capacity for excellence which is the foundation of their workplace expertise;

- Their occupation—the application of their talent in the workplace;

- Their industry—the venue in which they work with their talent; and

- Their ancillary skills—the complementary capabilities that will enable them to use their talent in the widest possible range of jobs and work situations.

THE NEW AMERICAN LAND RUSH

The menu of learning opportunities in the modern world of work is both long and varied. For that reason career activists are perpetual students, in the workplace as well as outside it. They continuously upgrade both their talent and their ability to put it to work. They do so, however, not to grab a bigger paycheck or take another step up the career ladder, but because they know that the greater their capacity to excel on-the-job, the more of their gift they will come to know. And, the more that happens—the deeper and richer their experience of working with and at their talent—the happier they will be.

Those who don't yet think of themselves as career activists have also begun to practice this fundamental aspect of activism. This more general commitment to development was reinforced and expanded by the ruthless Darwinian selection of the Great Recession. News reports and even some preliminary studies confirm that a significant number of American workers have now seen just how unfit they are for the modern workplace and are taking steps to acquire the occupational strength required to survive and prosper there.

For example, an informal survey conducted in 2009 by the American Association of Community Colleges found that enrollment among its members was 2-to-27 percent higher than a year earlier. Graduate as well as undergraduate programs at four year colleges and universities also saw significant increases. Indeed, the number of people taking the Graduate Record Examination in 2009 rose 13 percent from 2008, reaching a record high of 670,000 people.

Many of these prospective students are entering altogether new career fields. They are leaving behind the airline, automotive, financial services and other sectors of the economy that were hit hard by the economic downturn. They are abandoning occupations that have been ravaged by new technology or the in-and-out fads of consumers. And, they are shutting down their search for jobs on which they've relied for years but are now being shipped overseas to be done by cheaper workers.

Whatever the specific situation, these proto-career activists are taking their future into their own hands because they now realize that there is no security at the hands of their employers. As with the great American land rush of the 19th Century, they have set out in the 21st Century to stake their own claim to the American Dream. They are pushing their capacity for excellence out and up in order to create a more fulsome and reliable prospect for themselves and their families.

This vast migration to self-development is not limited to those who have been hardest hit by the Great Recession. A large number of employed Americans have begun to head back to school. These career activists aren't motivated by a pink slip, but by an unflagging commitment to express and experience more of their talent. They are determined to hone their excellence to an even higher state of perfection.

In a nation that is often accused of being self-satisfied and unwilling to sacrifice, they trudge off to after-work education programs and log onto weekend seminars. They invest their non-work time in making their work time better. At Bunker Hill Community College in Boston, for example, classes now run until 2:30 in the morning just to accommodate the demand. Other institutions are running as late or even later, and still others are starting classes before the sun even comes up so students can attend before their commute to work.

The seeds of this activism were planted during the "jobless recovery" that followed the dot.com bust and recession. The red ink may have stopped flowing among employers, but the effects of the economic downturn were still writing chapters of pain and frustration in the workforce. A lot of people were out of work, and many were having a very hard time getting themselves reemployed. Economists declared that 2001 marked the beginning of the nation's recovery, but according to the U.S. Bureau of Labor Statistics, almost 16 million Americans would experience unemployment at some point during that year.

At the same time, the U.S. Department of Education counted more than 92 million people enrolled in adult education programs. That figure represented over half of the American workforce. Even if all 16 million of the nation's unemployed workers were back in school, there would still have been an astonishing 76 million employed Americans who were trudging off to work each day and then off to school each night and weekend. Even if that figure were adjusted to account for the participation of retirees and for coursework that was unrelated to the world of work, it would represent an extraordinary commitment to career activism through self-improvement.

THERE IS NO AGEISM IN CAREER ACTIVISM

Career activists embark on this development for a very different reason than that which typically motivated mid-career education in the 20th Century. Unlike the corporate men and women who preceded them, they aren't taking courses to please or placate their boss. They aren't trying to position themselves for a raise or to take the next step up on some career ladder. Those outcomes may happen, but today's career activists are investing the time and making the effort to improve themselves because they want to express and experience more of their talent at work.

They are striving to become a better version of themselves so that they can reach for ever higher peaks of performance. They are reformatting themselves so they can better realize the dream encoded in the American culture. They are walking into real and virtual classrooms to prepare themselves for their pursuit of Happiness.

This commitment to self-development as a strategy for security and satisfaction at work is something new and different, at least among many American workers. It is not, however, being driven by the traditional trend setters in American culture—its youth. While many Millennials and Gen Xers realize that they still have much to learn about themselves and their talent, it is their parents who have been driven to the forefront of this movement.

The 2008 recession forced countless Baby Boomers to realize just how little they had learned about or used their talent at work. It shoved them out of comfortable jobs and established careers and made them confront the hidden decay in their expertise. And, while some have given up and gone into retirement, many more have decided to remediate themselves. They aren't giving up on their careers but instead, are going back to school to refurbish their capability.

An AARP survey, for example, found that one-out-of-six Americans over the age of 50 is now heading off to the classroom. When the respondents were asked why, almost half said to "sharpen skills on the job," That response was two times greater than any other reason given. In effect, the myth of the out-of-date, out-of-step, out-of-luck geezer in the workforce is just that—a myth.

Career activists have wrinkles as well as unlined faces. Their eyes are just as likely to reflect the rough and tumble of years gone by as they are to shine with anticipation at the years ahead. The workplace may still be rife with the disease of ageism, but the Career Activist Republic is not. Its culture acknowledges that talent inevitably morphs with age, but it never, ever goes away.

FROM UNEMPLOYMENT TO EMPLOYMENT INSURANCE

Career activists are found not only in every generation of contemporary America, but in every profession, craft and trade of the American economy, as well. They wear white collars, blue collars, pink collars, gray collars and every other kind of collar in the American workforce. They have been in the workplace for twenty-five or more years and for five years or less. Some hold an associate, bachelors or graduate degree while others have a state license or certification that requires continuing education. Whatever their status or talent, they are working as hard at their self-development as they are at the success of their employers.

They are undertaking this development on their own because they believe it is their responsibility to do so. They will take advantage of government tax credits and other assistance wherever they can, but they will do the rest themselves. They will invest the time, the energy, the commitment, and when the government's support falls short, the money to make it happen. They are, in effect, the venture capitalists of personal excellence.

This commitment to self-development is also driven by the view that government support is a band-aid, but not a cure for being out of work. It provides temporary unemployment insurance payments and job search support. It helps working men and women put food on the table, but—as millions of the long-term unemployed in the country can testify—it does not enable or empower them to succeed in today's evolving economy.

For that reason, a career activist believes they must create their own insurance—not for unemployment, but for employment. They engage in continuous self-development because they know that the perfection of their talent is the only real guarantee of a paycheck available in today's workplace. It alone ensures that they will be able to find work in a job of their choosing and to excel at it. And, it is that excellence—not the promises of employers or the contracts of unions or the assistance of the government—which provides the resilient and reliable security they seek. And deserve.

The alternative—holding their talent in check or holding it back from its fullest realization—is both a roadblock to satisfying work and the riskiest kind of behavior in today's workplace. And, career activists are determined to avoid both. They are curious about the potential of their gift and about what it might be trained to do. And, they are determined to protect themselves with a talent strong enough to ensure their continued employment, whatever the gyrations of the nation's economy.

More than that, however, they are respectful of their talent and committed to nurturing it to its fullest dimensions. They are determined to be talented because they know they can and because they believe they must. It is their responsibility and the surest way forward toward the deep and enduring fulfillment America's Founding Fathers called Happiness.

CHAPTER 12
The Application of Talent

The career ladder was a 20th Century device that enabled employers to control how individual ability was applied in the workplace. It forced working men and women into career pacifism by limiting the expression of their talent to positions selected by their employer and designed with the sole purpose of advancing its interests.

In some cases, those positions were also beneficial to the individual, but in many cases, they were not. The jobs may have paid well, they may have covered a person with a patina of seniority or importance, but all too often, they failed to engage their talent or give them an opportunity to be the best of themselves.

CAREER CASTAWAYS IN CORPORATE AMERICA

Despite its effectiveness as a workforce management tool, the career ladder began to lose its rungs during the last decade of the 20th Century. Pushed by growing domestic and international competition and intense shareholder activism, employers moved to cut overhead costs by downsizing corporate staffs, especially in the Human Resource

Department. This effort forced HR to eliminate some of its functions, and among the first to go was career management support for workers. Employers told employees *"You're on your own now. It's up to you to figure out which way to go with your career and to get yourself there."* In effect, the nation's workers became career castaways in corporate America.

In 2004, *The Free Agent Nation* was published to great acclaim because it offered what seemed to be a reasonable strategy for dealing with this new dynamic. People should set themselves up as Me, Inc., it declared, and hire themselves out as a free agent. The modern American worker will be a self-employed contractor who leases their talent out to this organization or that on a temporary basis. If employers will no longer manage a person's career, then each individual should hire and work for themselves.

The idea of self-employment was, at first blush, particularly appealing to a large segment of working Americans. It was, in essence, a blow for independence from their bosses, especially those who exemplified the Peter Principle or worse, were simply inept. While there are obviously many fine and caring supervisors in the American workplace, there are also numerous others who are ludicrously out of touch and totally unfamiliar with even the most basic tenets of leadership.

Just look at the antics of Michael Scott in "The Office". The program is popular because it portrays a business manager not as a deft captain of industry, but as the bumbling and self-delusional figure who is all too familiar to working men and women. While they can laugh at the show, however, the managerial myopia of their bosses can and does damage and even wreck their careers. Free agency, therefore, appeared to be both a smart defensive move and a way to set a more rewarding course for their work.

In addition, as own-your-own-business and work-at-home ads tout, being self-employed removes the most notorious of the wild cards in peoples' careers. It sets them up for the success they deserve by eliminating office politics and bureaucratic constraints on their good ideas and better ways of doing things. When people become their own boss, they finally have the freedom to accomplish great things. And, unlike in those multilevel marketing schemes, free agency didn't require them to buy a garage full of cleaning supplies or personal hygiene products.

THE FREE AGENT FALLACY

Self-employment seemed to provide everything a career castaway needed, at least until the bills came due. Despite all the hype and wishful thinking it generated, free agency simply didn't work for most Americans. Although the data are subject to different interpretations, the historical track record suggests that one-third of all small businesses in America fail. That's especially true of the smallest of small businesses—those started by sole entrepreneurs, including most free agents.

As if that situation weren't troubling enough, the failure rate appears to be accelerating. According to a 2009 study by the U.S. Small Business Administration (SBA), the number of defaults on SBA loans increased five-fold in just the four years between 2004 and 2008. And, that was before the Great Recession had begun to wreck its havoc on the economy.

The marketplace in a capitalist economy and the American business sector, in particular, is a highly competitive and fiercely unforgiving environment. The desire for independence does not change that reality. As a consequence, Me, Inc. fails more often—much more often—than it succeeds. Not because Americans aren't smart enough to run their own businesses, but because their hearts aren't in it. America isn't 19th Century Great Britain. It isn't a nation of individual shopkeepers. It's a nation of talented workers.

The Free Agent Nation, however, was only half wrong. It correctly focused on Americans' spirit of individualism and instinctive preference for self-control, but it failed to acknowledge the central paradox of the American Dream. The United States is arguably the most successful commercial nation in the history of the world, yet only a very small percentage of its citizens aspire to be business owners.

Most Americans do want to work for themselves, but they want to be employed by someone else. They yearn for their freedom, but they aren't excited about having to look for work day-in, day-out. They would like to meet and overcome worthwhile challenges at work, but they would rather not have to meet their own payroll. Indeed, in 2008 as the U.S. was rapidly falling into its deepest economic downturn in generations, the Small Business Administration recorded a barely noticeable 8 percent increase in one-person businesses.

This preference for employment by employers was also apparent in the aftermath of the 2001 recession. As the economy strengthened, survey-after-survey found that huge numbers of Americans were angered by how they had been treated during the downturn. A Conference Board poll taken in 2000, for example, found that only half of the American workforce (51 percent) was satisfied with their current work experience. That angst, however, did not prompt a massive outmigration from employers once the economy had recovered.

Workers said they were fed up and would jump ship just as soon as they were able. Most, however, stayed right where they were. *The Free Agent Nation* was roaring up the bestseller lists, but people weren't racing off into free agency. They were angry, to be sure, but they were also unwilling to take on the risk of change. They wanted employers to know they were unhappy with their treatment, but they also wanted to hang on to the paycheck those employers provided.

The simple fact is that most Americans are uncomfortable with disruption at work, and free agency creates a career of continuous disruption. Its short-term contracts and temporary assignments are far too unstable and risky to men and women with mortgages to pay and families to support. It's an appealing concept—and certainly it works for some—but for the majority of the workforce, the reality of free agency is a torture chamber of stress, anxiety and even fear.

FREE AGENTS BECOME PAID AGENTS TOO

Most Americans are most comfortable in long term employment situations. They want a decent job with some durability. Even if that durability isn't what it used to be. With so much change going on around them, they yearn for the comfortable familiarity of stability. Not only are they uneasy about starting a new job every couple of months, but many are all but terrified by the prospect of being responsible for landing their next gig and then the gig after that and the gig after that.

Career activism provides a way out of that dilemma. It empowers people to achieve their freedom without having to pay themselves for it. By working on themselves for themselves—by focusing on their talent and honing it to its highest state of refinement—they position themselves as a true human resource, rather than the faux version historically celebrated by chief executive officers. And, as with other valuable resources, organizations will actually compete with one another for access to them. In effect, career activists are free agents in the management of their own careers and paid agents who team up with employers to use their talent. They are employed by organizations, but work for themselves.

Although employers clearly participate in this new employment model, their role in no way undermines a career activist's independence or freedom of movement. Indeed, a career activist's commitment to self-improvement and the perfection of their talent creates a safe passage zone. The resulting state enables them both to choose among employers and to implement those choices in their career.

Career activists make such a significant contribution at work that they need not accept the first employment opportunity or any employment opportunity that comes along. More often than not, they don't even have to look for a job. Employers seek them out, and that urgent demand gives them their pick of both employers and assignments.

In effect, career activists replace the unreliable job security that employers have historically promised with a new and more durable form of workplace protection they create for themselves. They resurrect an American trait that is deeply ingrained in the nation's culture, but all too often pushed aside in the omnipresent prosperity of modern times. They accept, they practice and they relish self-reliance. They revert to being dependent on themselves. And, it's that sense of personal responsibility which guarantees their independence. It detaches them from the ever-shifting fortunes of employers in the 21st Century.

Self-reliance, however, does not disconnect career activists from workplace practicality. Whether it's the local deli, a department store in the mall, a manufacturing plant in the industrial park or an international corporation with center-city offices, these organizations own the jobs. Career activists, therefore, aren't free of employers; they are free of their dependence on any one employer. They aren't free agents; they are "freed agents." Their talent—if it's at the state-of-the-art and generously applied on-the-job—ensures that they can always be employed and always in a job of their choosing.

THE ALL-IN-ONE PACKAGE

In the 20th Century, American workers sought to protect themselves with contracts and the assurances of employers. They relied on the written and spoken word of others to ensure their continued employment. In the 21st Century, career activists protect themselves with their own talent. Their actions on-the-job create a contribution so significant that employers rely on them to succeed.

Career activists don't husband or hold back on the use of their talent in the workplace. They don't reserve it for a rainy day or restrict how much of it they provide to their employer each day. They deliver a daily return on an employer's investment in the application of their talent, a return that is denominated in excellence on-the-job.

T hat dedication to excellence—to using their talent to its maximum capacity on-the-job—is the trademark of career activists. They don't go to work as Me, Inc., but rather as Me™. And that signature brand positions them as the extraordinary contributors in an organization. They are the ultimate "do more with less" employee. They provide both superior productivity and high performance all in one package.

The application of talent creates a protective coating for the employer, one that is critical to its success in today's economy. Like a hardy but handsome veneer, it enables an organization to resist the turbulence in the marketplace and to stand out from its competitors. In a very real sense, career activists paint their employers with excellence. They are artists of workplace talent, and their brush strokes define the products and services of those organizations.

While obviously metaphorical, this image brings the impact of career activists into sharp relief. Their contribution is as genuine and visible as a coat of paint. And, their impact can be similarly measured.

Yahoo! Answers reports that *"Quality latex paint is normally applied about 4 mils thick and dries at 1.5 mils thick. A mil is 1/1000 of an inch."* Therefore, a career activist's daily application of talent creates a protective and vibrant covering that is over a quarter inch thick in just six months, over an inch thick in less than two years and almost a full foot thick (11.7 inches to be exact) at the conclusion of a 30-year career.

This accretion of value is apparent both in an organization's operations and at its bottom line. A 1997 study by the consulting firm McKinsey & Company found that a high performing worker was 50-to-100 percent more productive than a mediocre one. Unlike so much of what happens on the people side of business, the impact of a career activist's work can actually be recognized and measured by financial management tools. Even the CFO can see and appreciate it.

USING TALENT DOESN'T USE IT UP

While a person's application of their talent makes them more valuable to employers and thus enhances their security, career activists actually have another and stronger motivation. They use their talent because doing so improves it and them. They view each task, each assignment, even each problem they encounter as a worthwhile and personally beneficial test.

They believe that being challenged induces them to perform at their peak, to reach for new limits of excellence in their work. Applying their talent enables a career activist to be talented. It provides a way for them to experience their capacity for excellence. And that experience, in turn, enriches their sense of purpose and self-esteem in the workplace.

This growth occurs in two separate waves.

- **The first wave is direct.** Career activists do their best as they understand their best to be at any point in time, and that excellence promotes a deep and lasting sense of personal accomplishment.

- **The second wave is indirect.** From time-to-time, career activists will confront challenges that force them to tap reserves of talent they didn't even know they had, and that expression of their best gives them a greater appreciation of their gift's potential and potency.

There is, however, an important caveat to this virtuous two-fer. A person must do the right work in order to deepen and mature their talent. Said another way, the application of a person's talent on-the-job is their pathway to self-fulfillment and Happiness, but only if the work is worthy of their talent. The content of it must engage them, and its outcome must be meaningful to them. If it's not, if their talent is underused or misused, it will—just as an unexercised muscle does—weaken and eventually wither away.

Career activists understand this imperative. They move from one employment opportunity to another, but only to those where the work they do and the conditions under which they do it bring out the best of their talent. They do not accept jobs—no matter how well they pay, how short the commute they require or how prestigious the employer that offers them—if the tasks involved:

- cannot draw deeply on their talent. Career activists want to do what they do best—to perform work that uses only their talent and to excel at that work only by using the fullest dimensions of their talent.

- cannot produce outcomes they perceive to be important, inspiring and ethical. Career activists want to make a difference with their talent—to contribute to an outcome or mission that matters to them and makes them proud.

or

- cannot be effectively accomplished. Career activists want to succeed in their assignments—to work for employers that support them with the necessary resources and priority to do their best work.

THE AMBITION OF CHAMPIONS

Career activists work to be a champion in their chosen field. Their definition of championship, however, is unlike that traditionally associated with competitive endeavors. They aren't trying to best others in order to win the World Series or to medal in the Olympics or to be crowned a Grand Chess Master. They may earn such recognition—indeed, they often do—but their goal isn't to be better than everyone else in their line of work. Their sole purpose—their ambition—is to be the best of themselves.

They limit their employment, therefore, to situations that challenge and test them. They avoid jobs where they can skate by. They aren't interested in being mediocre. They don't want to perform at a level less than their best simply because an employer will tolerate it. To do so, in their view, would be letting themselves down. They know they have been blessed with a special gift, and they want to express and experience it in their work.

While this perspective is decidedly self-serving, it just as clearly benefits employers. It enables an organization to employ workers who are committed to contributing on-the-job. Contracts may codify that outcome, but it is the dedication of each career activist which guarantees it. Their personal commitment to peak performance maximizes the return an employer earns on its investment in them. Employers are bottom line dwellers, and career activists feed their insatiable appetite for results by bringing their excellence to work every day.

> Career activists apply their talent without let up and without fail. They do so because they believe that is the only way they can become a whole version of the champion within them. Consciously or unconsciously, they see their workplace persona as unfinished and therefore unfulfilled. They are good at what they do, but they are convinced they can be better.

Career activists aren't interested in climbing up some employer's career ladder but set themselves off on another, far more personal course. In effect, they reset their aspiration. Success isn't a promotion or a pay raise, but the ever greater realization of their inherent potential. It is the application of as much of their capacity for excellence as they can accomplish in their career.

CHAPTER 13
The Management of Talent

Aperson becomes a career activist by making a conscious decision to do so. Career activism doesn't happen by accident or by serendipity. It doesn't happen by preordained destiny or through the intervention of a benefactor. It occurs because an individual decides that he or she will place the perfection of their talent at work above everything else in their career and then acts to realize that goal.

DOING IT ON ONE'S OWN

A career activist holds the conviction that the traditional markers of progress at work are no longer compelling achievements for them. They decide that they will not be motivated by a pat on the back or even a pot of gold. They liberate themselves from the seduction of employer-based signs of success, not because they are indifferent to those accomplishments, but because they believe they can do better.

These employer-based accolades include being:

* selected for promotion within the organization;

- recognized as the "employee of the month, quarter or year;"

- rewarded with an above average pay raise;

- singled out for an end-of-year bonus;

or

- invited to an all-expense-paid excursion to some luxurious vacation spot.

Career activists are very good at what they do, so they frequently earn these awards and prizes. Such recognition, however, is not what inspires them. Conventional signposts of advancement are parceled out by employers, and career activists are determined to celebrate success on their own. They want to feel the sense of pride that comes from doing their best work. They seek to experience the fulfillment that is achieved by applying their talent to worthwhile challenges. And, they are determined to spend their career expressing their capacity for excellence in their very own pursuit of Happiness.

Career activists can arrive at this commitment to self-more service at any age and at any point in their career. It can happen when a person is 52 and claims their independence from parental corporations or when they are 22 and liberate themselves from hovering helicopter parents. All that's required is the assertion of independence.

Career activists decide that they can, they must and they will become the master of their career so they aren't left to imagine what they could have become. They set its direction and pace, they appraise its progress, they make adjustments when appropriate, and they acknowledge and celebrate what is accomplished. They do it all, and they do it on their own.

They are humble enough to accept a helping hand when they need it. And, they are self-confident enough that they don't need a clapping hand in order to feel complete. They do not disavow the traditional symbols of success; they simply strive to go beyond them—to reach continuously for more of their own excellence and the fulfillment that unique accomplishment provides.

REDEFINING EMPLOYMENT AT WILL

The working person's assertion of independence is the major paradigm shift of the 21st Century American workplace. It does not, however, signal a rise in free agency or a wave of entrepreneurism. While more Americans will find themselves in those endeavors from time-to-time, their involvement with them will typically be transitory. Self-employment is not the ultimate state they seek. It is a passage that their personal circumstances or the economy may force them to negotiate, but only as an interruption in their preferred modality. As soon as their situation stabilizes, as soon as the opportunity presents itself, most will return to employment by employers. And when they do, it will be with a radically new set of values and expectations.

A free and independent workforce resets the employment contract in America. It redefines "employment at will." The courts have not yet recognized this new reality, but to legions of American workers, it has already and irrevocably changed the way they work.

Today, employment at will no longer means that employers may hire and fire their employees whenever, wherever and however they want. Instead, the term now describes an environment in which the nation's working men and women can determine with whom they will team up in the use of their talent and under what conditions. Each individual will decide when, where, and how they will excel. Hence, it's their will that defines the relationship, not the employer's.

With the advent of this new employment contract, career activists are employed by an organization, but they do not work for it. They work with employers and for themselves. They do not sell their labor to or become the indentured servants of an organization. They are its business partner—an equal party in a joint venture.

Neither the career activist nor the employer expects that arrangement to last forever, but under the new definition of employment at will, termination can occur whenever it fails to benefit either of the parties. The moment that equal advantage ends, the arrangement will be dissolved. And, that step is as likely to be taken by the career activist—if they are the underserved party—as it is by the employer.

The benefit of any given arrangement is determined by the extent to which it contributes to the goals of the organization and each career activist. For the employer, the arrangement must support the accomplishment of its mission, whether that's providing a quality product or service or meeting the financial expectations of its shareholders or both. For the career activist, in contrast, the arrangement must support their attainment of the personal satisfaction and self-respect that come from doing their best work.

The "best work" of career activists occurs when they are employed at their talent and thus able to excel in an activity that is both engaging and meaningful to them. It can be achieved in any profession, craft or trade and in a wide variety of employment situations. It is also never static, but instead morphs to reflect the circumstances and requirements that exist at different stages in a person's career. In effect, "best" is individually defined and thus a personal or internal measure of success.

Hence, a person is a career activist and performing their best work if they are:

- A master plumber who takes great pride in their ability to solve a customer's household problem quickly and effectively;

- A civil engineer who gets up every day and looks forward to creating new structures that have both strength and beauty;
- A work-at-home Mom who makes it a priority to stay current in her workplace occupation even as she ferries her kids to soccer and helps out at their school;

- A professional baseball player who practices the skills of his trade every day even though he will never be recognized as an All Star or record setter;

- A customer service person who feels accomplished by being able to solve others' problems or answer their questions, regardless of how impatient or rude they might be.

A person is not doing their best work, on the other hand, if they are:

- A derivatives trader who works 80 hour weeks simply to make enough money to enjoy a luxurious lifestyle outside the workplace;

- A government bureaucrat who plods along in the same job in the same agency for twenty-five years solely to earn a pension after they retire;

- A job seeker who sits in front of a computer all day long and sends out application-after-application to jobs for which they aren't qualified and in which they aren't really interested;

- A professional baseball player who takes steroids or any other banned substance just to be recognized as an All Star or record setter;

- A manager or executive who is so focused on ensuring the success of their organization that they ignore other opportunities that would advance the development of their own talent.

THE DONUT HOLE IN AMERICA'S EDUCATION

After decades of enduring careers-for-consumerism, a growing number of Americans are now realizing that they deserve more out of their work. Jolted from their credit card addiction by the Great Recession, they have—often without recognizing it—begun to move toward career activism. Instinctively, they are recasting themselves as persons of talent.

These newly reformed workers are now exploring themselves to discover their capacity for excellence and nurturing that gift to prepare themselves for peak performance in their chosen field. They are investing the time and effort to develop their talent and working assiduously to apply it on-the-job. They are doing all the right things and still, they are seeing their careers weaken and even come to a halt. What they lack is a knowledge of the principles and practices of career self-management.

An education in those principles and practices is essential to a healthy career in the modern age. It should, therefore, be a national priority to provide it to every American. It promotes their employment security and, as a consequence, the wellbeing of the nation. Yet, most Americans are denied access to such preparation. In fact, a grounding in career self-management is the donut hole in the U.S. educational system.

This preparatory gap exists because many American educators, but especially those in the towers of academe, lack any experience in or contact with the 21st Century world of work. They continue to stand by the same solution to employment they have been offering for the last seventy-five years. They tell students and their parents that a college degree provides all that's required for success in the workplace. And, that's simply not true.

The millions of Americans who hold Bachelors degrees, Masters degrees and even PhDs and who are now out of work, prove beyond any doubt that such a claim is, at best, hopelessly outdated and, at its worst, insidiously self-serving. While an education in a viable career field is clearly necessary in America's contemporary knowledge economy, it is insufficient to create or sustain a healthy career. What's missing is an equal level of individual development in career self-management.

Collegiate deans and department heads may deny it, but there is a body of knowledge and a set of skills that must be learned and mastered before a person can manage their own career effectively. Career self-management may not be a traditional field of study, but it is a modern prerequisite for sustained and rewarding employment. A person's success, therefore, depends upon their being an expert in both their profession, craft or trade and in the strategies and tactics of guiding their career in the modern workplace.

They must be able to:

- set near, mid and longer-term goals that are meaningful to them and good for their career;

- determine the preparation—the additional capabilities, experience or professional standing—required to achieve those goals;

- plan for and accomplish that preparation effectively even as they continue to contribute on-the-job or pursue new employment in a job search;

- assess—continuously and candidly—their day-to-day performance on-the-job as well as the progress they are making toward their goals; and

- make adjustments, as required, to ensure they are engaged in work that will draw on and expand their capacity for excellence.

This proactive form of career intervention is dramatically different from what many Americans experience. They have been brainwashed into thinking that an occupational certificate or a college degree or (best of all) both will provide job security. Their reality, however, is something else altogether. They are the educated unemployed, underemployed and unlikely-to-stay employed of the modern workplace.

The current career experience of many attorneys provides an illustrative case in point. According to news reports, the number of people taking the law school entrance exam rose dramatically in 2009. Not surprisingly, law school applications soared, as well. At schools ranging from Washington University in St. Louis and Harvard University in Cambridge to the University of Iowa's College of Law and the Golden Gate University School of Law, applications were up from 20 to over 40 percent.

While the majority of these students were coming straight from undergraduate schools, many others were already in the workforce and changing careers. Having evaluated their prospects of success in their current occupation, they had apparently decided that getting an education in the legal profession was a smart way to advance their career.

Unfortunately, however, they hadn't done their homework, or at least, all of it. They had studied enough to get accepted into law school, but not enough to assess their prospects for a career in the law. Even a cursory level of research would have revealed significant problems in the current job market for attorneys. It's now not only tough to find employment in the legal profession, it's also tough to stay employed.

The New York Times, for example, published an article in 2009 which described the hard times at many of even the most prestigious law firms. The piece introduced Daniel Lukasik, an attorney with a Website called Lawyers with Depression. The name, itself, suggests that a career in the law may not be the safe harbor many people thought. The newspaper's account of Mr. Lukasik's experience brought that reality into clear focus:

> **" Mr. Lukasik recently received a call from a man who said he was a fifth-year associate in Manhattan who complained that he felt expendable even though he was a top performer.**
>
> **He said to me, 'What more do I have to do?' Mr. Lukasik recalled. 'I'm billing a large amount of hours, I'm a team player,' but he said it's very possible he might lose his job. And he was a Yale graduate, at a top-20 firm."**

This law firm associate was paralyzed by his sense of betrayal—by the feeling he had that his education and occupation had let him down. He had assumed—worse, he had been duped into believing—that because he was doing all the right things, the world of work would treat him right. He was simply unable to comprehend or accept that the workplace has its own set of rules and that those rules are not the same as the rules which govern a profession. Not only was his career in jeopardy, but he lacked the skills and knowledge to act in a way that would enable him to recover and land on his feet.

CAREER SELF-MANAGEMENT: NOT BY THE BOOKS

The career self-management donut hole emerges early in the education of America's workers. During high school, students are normally placed in one of two developmental tracks: a vocational path where they learn the basics for gaining employment in a craft or trade or a college-bound path where they acquire the foundation for gaining admission to higher education. Their entire secondary school experience is then limited to coursework which advances them toward those ends. None of the students, regardless of the track they're in, learn how to pick a career field or how to plan, direct and oversee their career once their education is complete.

Through missing link in education maimed millions of U.S. workers in the 20th Century; in the 21st Century, it could harm tens of millions more. America's students are now heading off to college each year as government officials and guidance counselors underscore the importance of higher education in the modern workplace. Once they arrive on campus, however, the knowledge they acquire is only a fraction of what they will need to build healthy and rewarding careers. They will graduate as career idiot savants: experts in their occupation or academic field, but without the self-management skills to succeed.

The simple fact is that America's institutions of higher education don't understand or even relate to careers that unfold outside the privileged sanctuary of tenure. Visit almost any American college campus today, and the career counseling assistance that's provided is housed in a "placement center" with a very different mission. Ignored until graduation and the real world of work is pressing on the horizon—typically sometime in a person's junior year but often as late as the second semester of their senior year—these offices focus almost exclusively on the rudiments of job search.

From the college or university's perspective, it's entirely appropriate that they do. Placement Centers are the front lines in the schools' efforts to reassure parents that their six figure investment in a child's education actually put them on a pathway to paid employment. To that end, they teach resume writing, interviewing skills and employer research. Their de factor mission is to help students find a job, not find the talent that will enable them to excel. They often have the expertise to perform effective counseling, but they lack the priority, time and staff to deliver it.

This situation is vastly different from what is now occurring in China. In that nation, every student is required to take a year-long course in career self-management. Called *Personal Mastery*, it is a prerequisite for graduation. These young men and women will never know the freedom and opportunities available in the American workplace, but they will know far more than their American counterparts about how to achieve career success.

Obviously, academic preparation is not the complete solution to acquiring the skills and knowledge of career self-management. Experience and the counsel of supervisors and mentors are also extremely important. Nevertheless, such an education establishes a critical foundation for success—just as it does in every occupation and career field—and the vast majority of American academic institutions have failed to provide it or even acknowledge its existence.

BUILDING A HEALTHY CAREER

Faced with this donut hole in their educational preparation, career activists must find a way to acquire the knowledge and skills required for effective career self-management on their own. There's no lack of information about what's required to conduct a job search—bookstore shelves groan with such titles—but unfortunately finding the prescription for a healthy career can be a challenge. Some rely on the insights of a mentor; others turn to career counselors and coaches; and still others invest in one of the small number of books that do address the subject.

Regardless of where or how they acquire their knowledge, however, all career activists manage their careers in the same way. In essence, they care for their careers exactly as healthy individuals attend to their physical fitness. In the 21st Century's turbulent and ever-changing world of work, a career activist knows that the health of their career will degrade if they don't focus on it every day. And, they accept that the other demands on their time—whether it's their current job or an ongoing job search—can distract them from that commitment so they set up and follow a personal plan to ensure they achieve "career fitness" and maintain it.

This approach to career self-management—visualizing it as the practice of career fitness—illustrates two traits that are now on the rise in the American population: self-reliance and personal initiative. For example, a 2009 Executive Mobility Survey conducted by the executive search firm BlueSteps found that an astonishing 75 percent of currently employed executives describe themselves as likely or very likely to consider taking a new job, despite the lingering effects of the Great Recession. They don't see themselves as anchored to their current employer and they are looking ahead to alternative employment opportunities that might better enable them to excel.

Almost three-quarters of the survey's respondents (74 percent) reported that they were looking for an employer that would more effectively serve their own career goals. They also wanted to work with an employer that had organizational values which were more tightly aligned with their own values. And, almost two-thirds of the respondents (64 percent) said they were searching for greater career development opportunities. In other words, they were seeking jobs that worked for them as well as for their employer.

Similarly, Catalyst, a membership organization for women in business, surveyed the graduates of top business schools in 2009—the people employers typically refer to as their "high potentials." It found that 23 percent had shifted to a new job from the one their employer had hired them to perform and 20 percent had actually left their employer to take a job with another organization. In effect, almost half of these top business school graduates were moving in the workplace to find employment situations that would enable them to use their talent more effectively.

And, this rising tide of personal initiative doesn't end there. Americans are also becoming more creative in pursuing their professional development. Historically, they have relied on their employers for additional education and training in their field of work. Today, they are acquiring this development on their own, enrolling in courses provided by academic institutions and commercial training companies, seeking out the counsel of their peers on social media Web-sites, and by joining, rejoining or sustaining their membership in professional associations and societies.

In fact, according to a 2010 survey conducted by McKinley Marketing, American workers are turning to professional associations and societies in growing numbers. Despite the effects of the economic downturn, almost half of the respondent organizations (44 percent) actually saw an increase in membership over the past five years and another quarter (23 percent) saw no decline.

Such proactive approaches to career self-management are the road signs of career activists at work. They signal the emergence of America's workers from a decades-long stupor of dependence on employers. They affirm their belief in their individual capacity for excellence. And, they stake their claim to full citizenship in the Career Activist Republic.

At the moment, only a relatively small segment of the American workforce has recognized the implications of what they have done. They have, in effect, declared their independence in the workplace, but are not yet aware of their personal sovereignty. They have set themselves free, but don't yet feel the full scope of that freedom.

That will shortly change. The moment for workplace democracy has arrived. As the benefits of this new and revolutionary form of active self-government become more visible—as its opportunity for true Happiness is realized—the consciousness of what America's workers have now achieved will grow and grow. The band of colonists will swell. And, their multiplying vision will refresh and enlarge the American Dream.

CHAPTER 14
The American Birthright

The United States of America has long been viewed as a land of opportunity. This sense of possibility invigorated the American Dream from the earliest days of the nation. It has drawn and continues to draw millions of people from around the globe, men and women who seek to better themselves and their families, who crave the fulfillment and pride of personal accomplishment.

These "huddled masses yearning to breathe free" testify to the potent power and promise of that vision. Whether they learn of it in English or Spanish, in Chinese or Russian or Swahili, the American Dream entrances and beckons them with a virtually irresistible force. They will arrive legally if they can and illegally if they can't. They will stand in line for visas and stand on cold street corners without them just for a chance to work in America.

No other place on earth witnesses such a disparate and determined inflow of humanity. The Irish and Italian arrivals at Ellis Island, the boat people of Cuba and Vietnam, the Chinese and Indian students who scramble for post-graduation work permits, and the illegal immigrants from Mexico and Haiti and Guatemala—all are unique to the United States of America. And, all are drawn by the imperfect, but genuine opportunity encoded in the American Dream.

Opportunity, however, is only real if it is accompanied by hope. The conventional view, of course, is exactly the opposite. Social scientists will argue that hope cannot long survive without opportunity. And that, undoubtedly, is true. But hope is a kind of palindrome. It doesn't read the same in two directions, but it does work that way. Hope depends upon opportunity, to be sure, but hope refreshes opportunity, as well.

And it is that dual directionality which makes the Career Activist Republic a uniquely American phenomenon. There is extraordinary opportunity elsewhere around the world—you can find it in China, certainly, and in India, Kuwait, Brazil and Germany. But, only in America do you have a culture of hope. Hope is the nation's spiritual heritage, and that heritage is one-of-a-kind.

The dictionary defines hope as "a feeling of desire for something and confidence in the possibility of its fulfillment." The opportunity of America is so outsized because the nation's hope is similarly unconstrained. It is the birthplace of the "can-do" spirit. America is the home of self-made millionaires and mom and pop businesses that put kids through college. It is where serial entrepreneurs flourish and garage-based businesses grow into global giants.

That hope, however, is beginning to feel unanchored. Thanks to a terrible recession and a recovery with fewer jobs and more demands in the jobs that do exist, America's exuberant optimism seems increasingly unwarranted and even naive. And, thanks as well to crooked but unrepentant bankers, greed-soaked traders and unethical executives, the nation's confidence in the level playing field of genuine possibility feels unjustified and even potentially harmful.

Today, America's working men and women have to struggle to find the opportunity that once was everywhere around them. They now must search for what had previously been theirs simply for the taking. And that unaccustomed effort—itself discomforting—is forcing them to adjust their expectations and their behavior. The expansive America they grew up with, counted on and believed in has suddenly grown unfamiliar and apparently much less robust.

CHANGING THE AMERICAN SUCCESS STORY

While pessimism and even a sense of futility are certainly understandable given the shocks the nation has endured, the United States of America remains a land of opportunity <u>and</u> a nation of hope. It still harvests a more open and fulsome prospect than any other place on the planet. It remains the world's breadbasket of possibilities. Whatever its problems, the USA continues to produce a rich outpouring of new ideas, creative solutions and innovative breakthroughs on which its citizens can and will continue to build their futures.

This resilience, however, doesn't mean that opportunities are static. They have changed and significantly so. They are now different in both their context and content. They will not be fulfilled of their own accord or at the direction of a person's employer. Today's opportunities are an individual accomplishment, and only the individual can make them come true. Further, they cannot be realized with a willingness to work, but instead require a determination to excel. They are not earned with labor, but with talent.

As monumental as that paradigm shift is, the greater change is the one it causes in the way individual success is achieved. American workers have generally been critical of those who feel entitled to the benefits of prosperity. They have little patience for those who won't work or work hard enough to achieve their goals. And yet, many of those same workers have unconsciously viewed a rewarding work experience as their right. They would never describe themselves as privileged, but deep down inside, they believe they deserve the reasonable standard of living a successful career provides. That outcome, they are convinced, is guaranteed to them as citizens. And now, they have been forced to acknowledge that it isn't.

Americans are promised the pursuit of Happiness, not Happiness, itself. The nation doesn't pledge to provide them with "a good and decent job" like some Hooverian "chicken in every pot." They aren't even guaranteed employment. And, there is no right to a middle class standard of living and certainly not to an income large enough for a four-bedroom home and a late model car in the garage.

In the modern economy of the United States of America, working men and women must actively work at their pursuit of Happiness. Whether they are employed on the assembly line or in a line of cubicles, they must act to find appropriate opportunities for their talent, they must act to prepare their talent to excel at those opportunities, and they must act to apply their talent on-the-job. And then, they must act to repeat that cycle over and over again.

This activism is the new dynamic in the American success story. It changes the pathway to the American Dream. The new course may chafe at people's well worn habits and comfortable assumptions, but that rub doesn't erase the goodness it provides them. Career activism is the verb of individual fulfillment. It is means by which a person moves him or herself from the dream they hold within them to the reality they and their family live out in the United States of America.

No less important, the collective impact of those realized individual dreams is a national reconstitution. The American Dream is being transformed into America's Dream. Career activism revitalizes the entire nation's opportunity. It sinks a wellhead of occupational restlessness that feeds energy and innovation into the workplace. The drive of each career activist, in effect, pushes the possibilities of everyone to an ever high level.

No matter how difficult or discouraging the times may be, Americans can be confident of both their present and their future. The opportunities may be different, but they still exist and multiply every day. The American Dream is as vibrant in the 21st Century as it was in the 20th Century.

Today, however, the Dream is being reclaimed by those who actually create and sustain it. It is no longer defined by industry trade groups and retail merchants. It is not home ownership or a European sports car or a country club membership. The people's vision of America's promise is more precious and enduring than all of those things, and it is now the ascendant faith of the nation.

What is America's Dream?

America's Dream is the freedom of each person to use their endowed talent in the pursuit of Happiness at work. It is the freedom they have to accomplish a single goal—to forge a future they cherish—by drawing on the genuine opportunity and enduring hope that happens only in the United States of America. That is their birthright, and its incarnation is the defining purpose of the Career Activist Republic.